ENVIRONMENTAL POLICY BENEFITS: MONETARY VALUATION

ORGANISATION FOR ECONOMIC CO-OPERATION AND DEVELOPMENT

Pursuant to article 1 of the Convention signed in Paris on 14th December 1960, and which came into force on 30th September 1961, the Organisation for Economic Co-operation and Development (OECD) shall promote policies designed:

- to achieve the highest sustainable economic growth and employment and a rising standard of living in Member countries, while maintaining financial stability, and thus to contribute to the development of the world economy;
- to contribute to sound economic expansion in Member as well as non-member countries in the process of economic development; and
- to contribute to the expansion of world trade on a multilateral, non-discriminatory basis in accordance with international obligations.

The original Member countries of the OECD are Austria, Belgium, Canada, Denmark, France, the Federal Republic of Germany, Greece, Iceland, Ireland, Italy, Luxembourg, the Netherlands, Norway, Portugal, Spain, Sweden, Switzerland, Turkey, the United Kingdom and the United States. The following countries acceded subsequently through accession at the dates indicated hereafter: Japan (28th April 1964), Finland (28th January 1969), Australia (7th June 1971) and New Zealand (29th May 1973).

The Socialist Federal Republic of Yugoslavia takes part in some of the work of the OECD (agreement of 28th October 1961).

Publié en français sous le titre:

L'ÉVALUATION MONÉTAIRE DES AVANTAGES
DES POLITIQUES DE L'ENVIRONNEMENT

In preparing the OECD Conference on Environment and Economics which was held in June 1984, a major effort for collection and analysis of data on the economic valuation of the benefits of environmental measures was undertaken. Following the conference, it was decided to prepare and publish a comprehensive report on this topic, incorporating the results of major studies which were being carried out in Europe and in the United States at that time.

A comprehensive survey of these studies has been achieved with the financial assistance of the Commission of the European Communities. A draft report was discussed in October 1986 at a workshop organised jointly by the Commission of the European Communities and the OECD Secretariat. A revised version was then examined by the OECD Environment Committee's Group of Economic Experts. This report is now published under the responsibility of the Secretary General.

Also available

AGRICULTURAL AND ENVIRONMENTAL POLICIES: Opportunities for Integration (1989)
(97 88 04 1) ISBN 92-64-13127-2   262 pages   £12.00   US$22.00   FF100.00   DM43.00

RENEWABLE NATURAL RESOURCES: Economic Incentives for Improved Management (1989)
(97 89 01 1) ISBN 92-64-13194-9   180 pages   £11.50   US$20.00   FF95.00   DM39.00

OECD ENVIRONMENTAL DATA/DONNÉES OCDE SUR L'ENVIRONNEMENT – COMPENDIUM 1987 (1987)
(97 87 02 3) ISBN 92-64-03960-5   366 pages   £20.00   US$42.00   FF200.00   DM86.00

WATER POLLUTION BY FERTILIZERS AND PESTICIDES (1986)
(97 86 02 1) ISBN 92-64-12856-5   144 pages   £6.00   US$12.00   FF60.00   DM27.00

Prices charged at the OECD Bookshop.

*THE OECD CATALOGUE OF PUBLICATIONS and supplements will be sent free of charge
on request addressed either to OECD Publications Service,
2, rue André-Pascal, 75775 PARIS CEDEX 16, or to the OECD Distributor in your country.*

ACKNOWLEDGEMENTS

This study was prepared by David W. Pearce and Anil Markandya, respectively Professor of Economics and Senior Lecturer in Economics at University College London.

They wish to acknowledge the contribution of J.-Ph. Barde.

TABLE OF CONTENTS

Chapter 1

INTRODUCTION

1.1. BENEFIT ASSESSMENT: SCOPE AND LIMITATIONS OF THIS REPORT

Benefit assessment is the widely accepted phrase for procedures which involve placing, as far as possible, a monetary value on the social advantages thought to accrue from improvements in natural and built environments. Its obverse is damage assessment, the monetary evaluation of the losses to society from environmental deterioration. It is important to establish the boundaries to the scope of this report. It is concerned solely with monetary evaluation techniques and with the associated procedures needed to engage in monetary evaluation. In order to place benefit assessment in perspective, Chapter 2 briefly surveys techniques which are aiding environmental decision-making but which do not involve monetary estimation. The rest of this Chapter, and much of Chapter 2 also, discuss the rationale for monetary assessment and the comparative merits of the alternative techniques that do not involve monetary valuations. But it is not the purpose of the report to engage in systematic analysis of non-monetary evaluation techniques. Nor does the report discuss the ways in which benefits assessment is actually used in decision-making. Some countries have elevated the technique to a formal status. In the United States, for example, Executive Order 12291 of February 17, 1981 makes all major regulations subject to "regulatory analysis". Within regulatory impact analysis (RIA) an estimation of the monetary value of benefits and costs of the regulation is essential. Outside of the United States no such formal status for benefit assessment exists. It is used in a fairly *ad hoc* way in a number of countries, and not at all in others. This report does not concern itself with an attempt to explain these contrasts. Its concern is solely to draw together the most recent and "best" of the benefit assessment work in an effort to provide a convenient synthesis for OECD Member Countries.

1.2. BENEFIT ESTIMATION AND THE IMPORTANCE OF ENVIRONMENTAL POLICY

The movement for environmental preservation and improvement has survived and grown despite a decade of economic recession. It has changed from being just a challenge to exploitative economic policy, to being a populist and pragmatic force, many features of which are already enshrined in legislation and constitutional intent. It is still true, however, that economically difficult times offer a challenge to the supporter of environmental improvement. Many of the gains from environmental policy do not show up in the form of immediate monetary gain; the benefits are to be found more in the quality of life than in any increment to a nation's economic output. But it is essentially an historical accident that some gains in human welfare are recorded in monetary terms in the national accounts and others are not. By and large, this is explained by the fact that the accounts measure gains to economic sectors in which property rights – whether private or public – have been well defined. The third party effects of economic activity – noise, air, pollution, water pollution etc. – do not show up in the accounts either because the ill-defined or absent rights to clean air, peace and quiet and pure water mean that no monetary transfer takes place between polluter and polluted, or because such transfers as do take place (e.g. through court action) are not part of the national accounting conventions. Thus environmental benefits tend to be less "concrete", more "soft" than market place benefits. The temptation is to downgrade them by comparison.

The widespread support for environmental policy can be seen as a rejection of this downgrading process. In reality, the environment is valued highly and one task in environmental policy is to record and measure these environmental values in whatever ways possible. This study is concerned with one such procedure for testing and measuring environmental values: the use of monetary indicators of "benefit". Its primary intention is to draw attention to a now substantial empirical literature which is concerned with monetary benefits in the belief that this rich source of information needs to be a focus of understanding in environmental policy. It also shows how benefit estimation can assist the regulatory process.

One potential source of confusion needs to be avoided at the outset. Some environmentalists would argue that protecting the natural environment and the man-made heritage is economically worthwhile in a more traditional sense. It is, they argue, a sound source of employment creation and is perhaps linked to positive

Table 1. **Pollution damage in the Netherlands**

In billions

	Cumulative damage to 1985		Annual damage 1986	
	Gld	US$	Gld	US$
Air Pollution	4.0 - 11.4	1.2 - 3.0	1.7 - 2.8	0.5 - 0.8
Water Pollution	n.a	n.a	0.3 - 0.9	0.1 - 0.3
Noise Nuisance	1.7	0.5	0.1	0.0
Total	5.7 - 13.0	1.7 - 3.5	2.1 - 3.8	0.6 - 1.1

Source: Netherlands Ministry of Public Housing, Physical Planning and Environmental Management, *Environmental Program of the Netherlands 1986-1990*, The Hague, 1985; and J.B. Opschoor, "A Review of Monetary Estimates of Benefits of Environmental Improvements in the Netherlands", OECD Workshop on the Benefits of Environmental Policy and Decision-Making, October 1986.

changes in technology and productivity. These claims are not investigated here. They have been extensively analysed elsewhere (OECD 1985). Thus, putting people to work on environmental tasks obviously creates employment if otherwise unemployed resources are utilised. But whether it is the most efficient way of creating employment is more debatable. Consider energy insulation schemes. They create jobs for people in the building and related industries. But what happens to the jobs that depend on the expenditure diverted by the insulation schemes? They may decline in numbers more than the insulation scheme jobs increase: it is a matter of empirical investigation.

The view taken here is that environmental policy may well have additional justifications in objectives such as employment but it has more compelling support in the revealed preferences of the population for environmental goods and services.

1.3. NATIONAL ESTIMATES OF POLLUTION DAMAGE AND THE BENEFITS OF CONTROL

It is possible to illustrate the way in which benefit estimation techniques have been used to measure the importance of damage to the environment and, the converse, the benefits of environmental policy.

Table 1 shows estimates for the costs of environmental damage in the Netherlands. Note that these are estimates of damage arising from pollution. A good many types of damage did not prove capable of "monetisation", so that, if the monetised figures are accepted, actual damage exceeds the estimates shown. Various techniques were used to derive the figures and considerable caution should be exercised in quoting or using them. They are, at best, "ball park" numbers. Nonetheless, they show that even measured damage is a significant cost to the economy – the totals shown for 1986 are 0.5 – 0.9 per cent of Netherlands GNP.

Table 2 presents the same type of estimates for Germany. Again, many items have not been valued and differing techniques are used to derive the estimates. The figures shown total to over DM 100 billion annual damage (about US$34 billion), the major part of which is accounted for by the disamenity effects of air pollution (which is likely to include some of the separately listed air pollution costs), and the effects of noise nuisance on house values. The figure of DM 100 billion is in accordance with the estimates of Wicke (1986). The important point is that, if the estimates can be accepted as being broadly in the area of the true costs, pollution damage was costing an amount equal to 6 per cent of Germany's GNP in 1985.

Table 2. **Pollution damage in Germany**

Annual figure

	1983/5	
	DM billion	US$ billion
Air Pollution		
Health (respiratory disease)	2.3 - 5.8	0.8 - 1.9
Materials damage	2.3	0.8
Agriculture	0.2	0.1
Forestry losses	2.3 - 2.9	0.8 - 1.0
Forestry recreation	2.9 - 5.4	1.0 - 1.8
Forestry – other	0.3 - 0.5	0.1 - 0.2
Disamenity	48.0	15.7
Water Pollution		
Freshwater fishing	0.3	0.1
Groundwater damage	9.0	2.9
Recreation	n.a	n.a
Noise		
Workplace noise	3.4	1.1
House price depreciation	30.0	9.8
Other	2.0	0.7
Total	103.0	33.9

Source: Adapted from data given in W. Schulz, "A Survey on the Status of Research Concerning the Evaluation of Benefits of Environmental Policy in the Federal Republic of Germany", OECD Workshop on the Benefits of Environmental Policy and Decision Making, Avignon, 1986.

Table 3 shows estimates for the United States from Freeman (1982) for the year 1978. However, in this case the figures are for damage avoided by environmental policy. That is, taking the total of $26.5 billion, the argument is that, in the absence of environmental policy, pollution damage would have been $26.5 billion higher in 1978 than it actually was. The total shown in Table 3 would be 1.25 per cent of GNP in 1978. The marked divergence between this figure and the percentage suggested for Germany is partly explained by the absence of estimates for noise nuisance, and by the very low figure for property value changes.

Table 3. **The benefits of pollution control in the United States, 1978**

$US billion

Air Pollution	
Health	17.0
Soiling and Cleaning	3.0
Vegetation	0.3
Materials	0.7
Property Values[1]	0.7
Water Pollution[2]	
Recreational Fishing	1.0
Boating	0.8
Swimming	0.5
Waterfowl Hunting	0.1
Non-user Benefits	0.6
Commercial Fishing	0.4
Diversionary Uses	1.4
Total	26.5

1. Net of property value changes thought to be included in other items.
2. At one half the values estimated for 1985.
Source: M. Freeman, *Air and Water Pollution Control: a Benefit-Cost Assessment*, Wiley, New York, 1982.

1.4. BENEFIT MEASUREMENT AND REGULATORY POLICY

Apart from acting as an indicator of the strength of environmental preference, benefit measurement has an essential role to play in regulatory policy through the use of cost-benefit analysis (CBA).

CBA is one of a number of decision-making aids. The main alternatives are surveyed in Chapter 2. CBA looks at the monetary value of benefits because of the need to compare them with the costs of a policy which are automatically expressed in monetary terms. In addition, monetary costs should reflect the value to society of the resources being used up. The requirements that benefits exceed costs before any policy can be deemed *prima facie* socially desirable is thus a requirement that the value to society of the benefits obtained be greater than the value of the resources used up by the policy. It is in this sense that CBA is a rational decision-making aid, based on principles of economic efficiency. It contrasts with other decision aids in that very respect. For example, if benefits cannot be measured in money terms, it will be necessary to resort to some judgmental assessment of them in relation to their costs. Such judgmental procedures are typical of environmental impact assessments, for example, or cost-effectiveness analysis, or decision analysis in general.

One strength of CBA is that it tries to avoid this judgmental component and treats costs and benefits in common conceptual terms. But it is also a much criticised technique. Many feel that comparisons of overall money aggregates tend to obscure more than they reveal. For example, it does not say anything about the incidence of the costs and benefits between different interest groups or social classifications. If overall present value aggregates are used, it will not say anything about the distribution of costs and benefits over time. In short, the attraction of "collapsing" the entire problem into a comparison of a few measures of costs and benefits is for many people a source of criticism. It so happens that much of the criticism of CBA is also criticism of the alternative procedures such as environmental impact assessment. There is for example an unavoidable requirement to assess the relative importance of impacts. Is employment more important than negative impacts on an ecologically sensitive area, do the poor count more than the rich? And so on. CBA tries to use the weights that are implicit or explicit in people's choices. Other techniques tend to resort to expert judgment or the judgment of those who have ultimately to make the choice. Neither alternative is without its problems.

Benefit estimation *is* uncertain, and it is not unusual to find competing and different estimates of benefits for a single policy or project. Again, this problem is common to all decision-aiding techniques, so that, in itself, it is not a powerful criticism. However, benefit estimation does reduce effects to a single figure, whereas alternative procedures tend to present an array of impacts. As a result, it is not always easy to identify why competing benefit estimates differ. This process of identification is easier with other techniques.

Finally, benefit estimation tends to concentrate on *economic efficiency* impacts only. These are important in the regulatory process if governments are to pursue efficiency in public spending. But there are many other goals in the regulatory process, as noted above. The tendency to focus on a single figure may obscure the fact that only one of the goals of public spending is being measured by the benefit estimate.

1.5. BENEFIT ESTIMATION AS AN ORGANISING PRINCIPLE

This study is not concerned to defend or criticise CBA. Whatever the use to which the results of a CBA are put, benefit measurement as an *investigative procedure* has taught us a great deal about the nature of the value of environmental improvement, for example that there are varying motives for placing values on the environment. In turn those motives have considerable implications for policy. One example can be given. It is tempting to think that, in the absence of moral or survival reasons for protecting environments, a particular area that is frequently visited should be subject to more protection than one that is less frequently visited. The benefits appear larger in the first case. In practice, we may find in the process of measuring those benefits that the second site should be preferred to the first. This may be because there are substantial benefits to those who do not visit the second site: they may simply prefer it to be left alone and their not visiting it may simply reflect this concern. It is possible, then, that the measured benefits to the second site are greater than the first. The essential point is that benefit measurement techniques have taught us a good deal about the nature of environmental preference, and it is not entirely clear that this understanding would have advanced without benefit measurement.

In much the same way, our understanding of the design of methods for implementing environmental policy would be much the poorer but for benefit measurement. The concept of a pollution tax for example was first described in the context of a theoretical model of pollution in which it was *assumed* that benefits and costs should be measured in monetary terms. While actual pollution taxes are still rare in environmental policy, the efficiency of different instruments for controlling pollution can still be measured in comparison to one designed to secure optimal net benefits. It may be objected that *a)* such an argument assumes that maximising net measured benefits is a "good thing" and *b)* that it still has not been established that it is necessary to measure benefits in monetary terms. The argument for supposing that the maximisation of net benefits is a good thing has already been indicated: it is a rational objective. The second argument is partly persuasive. But in practice we still need to know something about the approximate size of a tax and the approximately "right" level at which to set standards. Neither of these pieces of knowledge can be obtained in the context of rational environmental policy without some idea of the scale of money measured benefits. Once again, then, it is not necessary for benefit measurement to be exact for our argument to be sustained. What matters most is that we learn to think rationally about environmental issues through the process of economic analysis, and we argue that benefit measurement is one significant component part of that analysis. The process matters as much as the result.

1.6. THE CONCEPT OF A BENEFIT

The underlying purpose in attempting a monetary measure of benefits is to provide a check on the economic rationality of investing in environmental improvement. The cost of such improvements is measured in money terms and the monetary sum involved should approximate the value to society of the resource used up. Since resources are scarce it is important to establish that the gain from the policy exceeds the resource cost, and this can only be done by measuring the benefit in the same units as the costs. In fact expenditures should be undertaken until the extra benefits are just equal to the extra costs. In formal terms, marginal benefit should equal the marginal cost of providing that benefit. In turn, this equivalence meets the requirement that the scarce resources in the economy be used in their most efficient way, i.e. given a certain level of resources, the marginal benefit = marginal cost rule maximises the total net benefit that can be achieved with these resources. Clearly, in practice there can be no assurance that all benefits are measurable, nor is it possible to allocate resources so as to maximise net social benefits even if all benefits were measurable. Too many influences – e.g. political considerations – intervene. Nor do societies aim to maximise net benefits alone. They also consider other objectives such as fairness, national security and so on. Thus benefit measurement can only assist with a more limited aim of checking that the policy in question is an improvement in economic efficiency compared to the initial situation. Rather than achieving efficiency, then, benefit measurement helps us with the process of moving towards efficiency in terms of only one social objective, but an important one.

Moreover, it is important to understand that the concept of benefit is interpreted in a particular way. The basic idea is that "what people want" – individuals' preferences – should be the basis of benefit measurement. The easiest way to identify these preferences is to see how people behave when presented with choices between goods and services. We can reasonably assume that a positive preference for something will show up in the form of a willingness to pay for it. In turn, each individual's willingness to pay will differ. Since we are interested in what is socially desirable, we can aggregate the individual willingness to pay to secure a total willingness to pay. The willingness to pay (WTP) concept thus gives an automatic monetary indicator of preferences. While we can safely assume that people will not be willing to pay for something they do not want, we cannot be sure that WTP as measured by market prices accurately measures the whole benefit to either individuals or society. The reason for this is that there may be individuals who are willing to pay more than the market price. If so, their benefit received is larger than market price indicates. The "excess" that they obtain is known as consumer surplus.

Accordingly we can write the following fundamental rule:

WTP = *Market Price + Consumer Surplus*

The idea can be illustrated with the aid of a diagram showing a demand curve. Figure 1 shows that the market price, determined by forces of supply and demand in this case, is P*. Since it is not possible to charge a different price to each and every individual buying the good, P* becomes the market price for everyone. But individual A can be seen to be willing to pay a higher price Pa. Similarly, individual B is willing to pay a price Pb. The total amount of benefit obtained is in fact the entire area under the demand curve shown by the two shaded areas. The shaded rectangle is the total expenditure by individuals on this particular good, and the shaded triangle is the consumer surplus. The two areas together then measure total benefit.

The intuitive basis to monetary benefit measurement is thus rather simple. People reveal their preferences for things they desire by showing their willingness to pay for them. Market price is our initial guide to what people are willing to pay and hence total expenditure on the good is our first approximation of benefit received. But since

there will be people willing to pay more than the market price, and hence who secure a surplus of benefit over expenditure, total WTP will exceed total expenditure. What we seek in benefit measurement, then, is a measure of areas under demand curves.

As it happens, the strict requirements for areas under demand curves to measure benefits is more complicated than this. Demand curves of the kind shown in Figure 1 have the same income level as we move up or down the demand curve. Along such demand curves, known as Marshallian demand curves, income is held constant. We require that the individual's welfare, well-being or "utility" be held constant, which somehow means correcting the demand curve for the fact that utility varies as we move up and down the demand curve. Such adjustments have been worked out in the economics literature. Figure 2 shows the same demand curve as Figure 1 but this time P* falls to P≠ because of some change in the market. It will be evident that the price falls make the consumer "better off" because the total shaded area has actually increased. The gain from the price fall is shown by the heavy shaded area. Hypothetically, we can ask the consumer what he is willing to pay to secure the price fall so as to leave him as well off at P≠ as he was at P*. This measure, based on the income

Figure 1

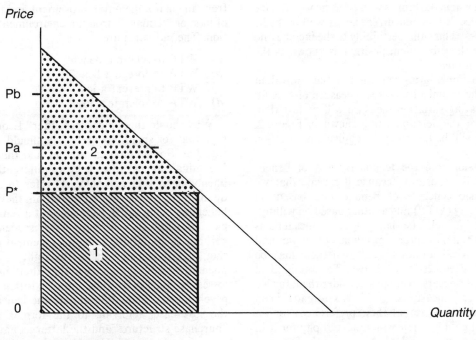

1 = Total expenditure
2 = Consumer surplus
1 + 2 = Total benefit

13

Figure 2

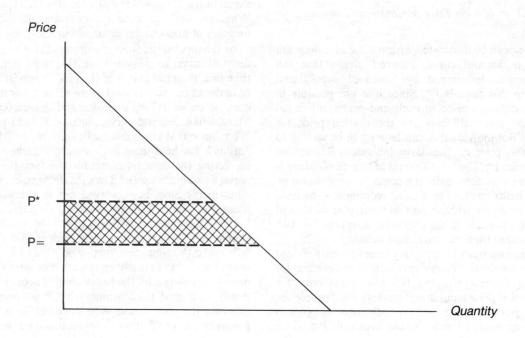

and relative price pertaining to P*, is known as the *compensating variation* measure of benefit. If instead we ask the consumer how much he would be willing to accept in order to forego the price fall, the relevant base point will be P≠. That is, the consumer will want a sum of money that will make him as well off as he would have been if the price fall had occurred, i.e. as well off as he would be at P≠. This sum, pertaining to the income and price levels at the subsequent position, is known as the *equivalent variation*.

Either the compensating variation or the equivalent variation is the technically correct measure of benefit. The compensating variation measure will be less than the area under the demand curve shown in Figure 2, which in turn will be less than the equivalent variation measure.

This digression into the technical basis of benefit measurement is important because it reveals that we have two basic concepts of benefit: one based on willingness to pay (WTP) and another based on willingness to accept (WTA). The theory of economics tells us that these ought not to differ very much, but, as we shall see, some empirical studies suggest that there may be marked differences between the two. To obtain some idea of why this appears to happen consider the intuitive basis of the two measures. WTP has already been explained: individuals reveal their preferences for an environmental gain by their willingness to pay for it in the market place (we consider in a moment the fact that most environmental goods and services have no markets). But we are often faced with the problem of how we

value an environmental loss. In that case we can ask how much people are willing to pay to prevent the loss or how much they are willing to accept in the way of compensation to put up with the loss.

In short, there will be two measures of benefit gained from an environmental improvement and two measures of loss, or "damage", from an environmental deterioration. The measures are:

a) WTP to secure a benefit;
b) WTA to forego a benefit;
c) WTP to prevent a loss;
d) WTA to tolerate a loss.

Why should these measures differ? Economic theory says that for small changes, they should be very close together. Some empirical studies find that they differ. Individuals appear to view losses differently to gains, a phenomenon that psychologists refer to as "cognitive dissonance". Given an initial position, they see an extra benefit as being worth so much, but a removal of some part of what they already have is seen differently, perhaps as containing some infringement against what they regard as being theirs "by right". Certainly, the phenomenon of asymmetry in the valuation of gains and losses in relation to some initial position is known to psychologists. They differentiate the benefit case from the loss case, referring to the former as having a "purchase structure" and the latter as having a "compensation structure". How the values differ in the two contexts depends very much on what is considered by the individual as being the "normal" state.

If WTA and WTP do differ significantly, then we have a problem for the measurement of environmental benefits. For many cases will involve the prevention of a loss rather than securing a benefit. It is likely then that the "compensation structure" will be more important in these cases than the "purchase structure". A policy of preventing the loss may not be justifiable if the measure of benefit is based on WTP to prevent the loss, but justifiable if the benefit is measured as WTA compensation to tolerate the loss. It seems fair to say that this issue is not resolved in the environmental economics literature. Psychologists express little surprise that WTP and WTA are not the same; some economists find that they differ in many studies; others find that they may converge if the study is formulated in a particular way, and economic theorists tend to dispute that WTP and WTA can differ so much simply because the theory says that they ought not to differ (and hence there must be something wrong with the empirical studies).

1.7   THE ABSENCE OF MARKETS

The preceding discussion assumed that the environmental good or service was directly marketed. In such cases the benefit measurement technique rests on the observation of market prices and the estimation of the demand curve, suitably adjusted to obtain a compensating or equivalent variation measure. But the vast majority of cases in the environmental context will comprise environmental benefits and losses for which there is no evident market. Thus clean air is not bought or sold in the market, nor is peace and quiet. Some environmental damages have a market aspect, even though there is no direct market in reducing the source or the damage. Thus, damage to vegetation from ozone pollution does show up in the market-place to some extent in that marketable crops are damaged.

There are three basic procedures for securing money measures of benefits in the absence of markets.

The first is to look for a *surrogate* market. This is a market in some other good or service which is influenced by the non-marketed environmental good. An example would be the property market. Houses are bought and sold on the property market, and one of the factors influencing the decision to buy or sell is the level of air pollution, level of noise, changes in aesthetic surroundings, and so on. This suggests that there may be some way to infer the values of the environmental services by an analysis of the housing market. Another example is the extent to which people's willingness to spend time travelling to a natural amenity site helps us to infer their valuations.

The second approach is to "create" a market by eliciting individuals' response to some form of questionnaire. Basically, individuals would be asked directly what they are willing to pay or accept. So long as their responses can be relied upon, with some acceptable margin of error, to reflect what their values would be if a real world market existed, this procedure will offer a rich source of information.

The third procedure mixes *physical linkage* information with either market or surrogate market valuation. An example would be the valuation of health damage. This involves establishing the statistical epidemiological link between "doses" of pollution and a "response" such as mortality or ill-health. This is the physical linkage part of the exercise. The next stage is to apply to the response some value per unit of damage done – an example would be a monetary value of life taken from studies of how people behave with respect to occupational mortality risks. Another example would be to find a dose-response relationship for air pollution and the erosion of building surfaces. The value of damage done could then be approximated by looking at the cost of accelerated replacement or repair of the building which is essentially a market value.

There are various other ways of classifying the techniques. Thus both the surrogate market and questionnaire approaches rely on behavioural responses for their information. (We may add laboratory style techniques as well, in which individuals' value responses are elicited through various stimuli.) The physical linkage approach does not rely on behavioural responses: the dose-response relationship that is sought tends to be outside the immediate control of the individuals in question, or involves no responses at all, as in the case of building damage. In practice, all kinds of responses may be intertwined – crop damage for example may be attenuated because farmers perceive the effects of the pollution and try to protect their crops' growth with added fertilizer. Individuals may try to avert noise nuisance by double-glazing, and so on. But what is important is that techniques do exist for finding values even though there are no obvious markets.

All techniques that rely on some eliciting of preferences will be referred to as *Direct Valuation* techniques.

Procedures that rely on dose-response relationships will be referred to as *Indirect Valuation*.

1.8.   UNCERTAINTY

Benefit measurement has to take place in the context of uncertainty. Two basic types of uncertainty exist.

The first type relates to uncertainty about the physical linkages in the environment system, and is thus particularly relevant to the indirect valuation approaches. The damage that acid deposition does to buildings, for example, is not known with certainty, so that the money estimates of the corrosion damage will themselves be subject to margins of error. The economic value of pure groundwater may be known with reasonable accuracy, but the physical modelling of groundwater flow and the dispersion of contaminants is not accurate. Models of air pollution dispersion have limited accuracy even for atmospheric pollutants, while for problems such as trace gas impact on stratospheric ozone, modelling remains very much in its infancy (though advancing rapidly).

The second type relates to the valuations themselves. As will be seen, many benefit estimation techniques rely on economic models which can be specified in various ways. The resulting valuations are themselves sensitive to the way the economic model is specified. Limited study may also have been made of revealed preferences so that there is added uncertainty due to limited development of the valuation technique.

The existence of uncertainty is not a reason for rejecting benefit estimation. Rather it is a justification for developing further the valuation techniques, and for collaboration between scientists and economists on the underlying physical linkage systems.

1.9. TIME AND DISCOUNTING

The benefits of environmental policy and the damages arising from environmental pollution and destruction need not be immediate. The irreversible loss of a natural habitat is immediate but its effects are felt for long periods of time. Some pollutants have effects on human health or wildlife only after time lags. Time is thus of central importance in benefit and damage estimation. We need to know how future damage is to be weighed against current damage, for example, and whether an investment that yields benefits only in the fairly distant future is worth carrying out now. Without going into detail, the general procedure in benefit estimation is to accept that, just as benefits are measured with reference to people's preferences, so people's preferences with respect to time must be accounted for. Since people tend to prefer their benefits now rather than later, and their costs later rather than now, a benefit or cost in the future should be *discounted*. The rate at which they are discounted is referred to as the *discount rate*. A discount rate of 10 per cent, for example, means that $1 of benefit next year is regarded as being worth $1/1.1 = $0.91 this year. A benefit of $1 in two years' time is regarded as currently being worth $1/(1.1)^2 = $0.83, and so on.

Discounting procedures and their rationale will be discussed in more detail in Chapter 6. For now it is only necessary to note that if the discount rate is greater than zero, implying a preference for the present over the future, benefits that occur very far into the future will appear insignificant. Similarly, and perhaps of greater concern, costs in the far future will also be insignificant. To see this, consider $1 million of cost in 50 years time. At a 10 per cent discount rate that cost is viewed as being worth now a sum equal to $1/(1.1)^{50}$, or less than 1 cent!

Armed with this very basic view of benefit concepts we are now in a position to apply them to environmental benefits and costs.

Chapter 2

BENEFIT ESTIMATION IN THE CONTEXT OF DECISION-MAKING

2.1. INTRODUCTION

Any rational decision-making process weighs up the advantages and disadvantages of a policy action. The way in which these advantages and disadvantages are compared vary according to the type of decision "rule" or "framework" that is used. But it is important to understand that all decision rules proceed by:

i) Defining gains and losses according to some objective or some set of objectives;

ii) Listing gains and losses;

iii) Measuring gains and losses in the same or different units;

iv) Using either explicit "importance weights" or implying such weights ex post by making a decision on the basis of *i)* to *iii)* above.

The types of framework widely advocated are:

a) Cost-Benefit Analysis (CBA);

b) Cost-Effectiveness Analysis (CEA);

c) Multi-Criteria Analysis (MCA);

d) Risk-Benefit Analysis (RBA);

e) Decision Analysis (DA);

f) Environmental Impact Assessment (EIA);

There is considerable debate about the relative merits of each of these techniques, much of it adding to the confusion rather than clarifying it. [However, for one interesting and useful summary, see Bidwell (1986).] Thus CBA is often thought to be ignoring uncertainty when in fact this aspect of decision-making is extensively analysed in the CBA literature. Similarly, CBA is criticised because it neglects the distributional incidence of costs and benefits, perhaps between social groups or regions. In fact many CBA studies incorporate distributional incidence analyses [for a survey see Pearce (1980)]. CBA is also criticised because of the attempt to "value the invaluable", for example by placing money value on human life or unique scenery. This latter criticism has more validity in respect to the uncertainty and complexity surrounding such valuations, but it tends to be directed at studies which do not honour the basic analytical foundations of CBA. As with all decision-aiding procedures, there is "good" and "bad" CBA. CBA certainly risks obscuring the nature of the various gains and losses by aggregating them and thus making them more obscure to the decision-maker. But this aggregation procedure comes about through the use of a common measuring rod, money, in the form of (shadow) prices. In turn, these prices are "importance weights" where the criterion of importance is usually (but need not be) economic efficiency.

What these prices reflect are individual preferences revealed or inferred by various techniques, but they could equally well be the preference of decision-makers (and often are in actual case studies). This rids us of a further misunderstanding about CBA – that it ignores benefits and costs that are better valued by the paternal concerns of the government. More fundamental is the concern, however, that *whatever decision rule we use, importance weights must be found.* CBA happens to use efficiency prices based on the idea that they act as guides to situations in which we can make "society" better off in terms of the preferred options of the individuals who comprise that society. It is less obvious what the rationale is for determining the importance weights in other techniques.

The preceding discussion can only touch on the debate between advocates of the differing decision rules. It highlights the role of CBA not because we wish particularly to defend it, but because as one of the "older" procedures it has been widely commented on and widely misunderstood. In what follows the similarity of the bases of each of the decision rules is shown and the differences that might lead to the use of one procedure rather than another are highlighted. We further show the role which benefit assessment plays in each.

2.2. COST-BENEFIT ANALYSIS

CBA proceeds by measuring, as far as possible, the costs and benefits of a policy or action. Since the resource costs of policies are invariably in money terms, comparison is undertaken by measuring benefits in money units. It is not necessary, however, that all benefits and costs be in money terms.

There are two fundamental features of CBA. First, along with other decision rules, it forces the analyst and the decision-maker to list the pros and cons of any action. This listing activity is perhaps the most important aspect of decision rules. Second, and interlinked with the first feature, the listing must reflect some prior assumption or decision about what it is that matters. In the economist's language, this prior decision is one of choosing the "social welfare function'. All that it means is that we decide what the ultimate goal (or goals) is (are) and then determine what it is that contributes to that goal. If, for example, the goal is utility or the welfare of humans, then anything contributing to gains in that welfare is a benefit and anything detracting from it is a cost. Care has to be taken not to double-count, nor to count as a benefit to society a simple transfer from one member of the community to another. Such transfers will be relevant when one is considering the distributional incidence of costs and benefits, however. The social welfare function in CBA thus assumes a value judgment – namely that individual preferences and their fulfillment are what matter. This is the basic value judgment of CBA. Any decision rule assumes one or more value judgments, so that criticism of CBA or any other rule on the grounds that it is "value loaded" is a rather basic misconception. What matters is that the value judgment be made clear. We can readily change it, for example by substituting a judgment to the effect that only the preference of some people matter. (Note that this is not equivalent to substituting decision-makers' preferences for individual preferences: the idea behind that approach is that decision-makers know better than individuals what is desirable in some circumstances.)

The basic rule of CBA is that a policy is a desirable policy if:

$$NSB = (B - C) > 0$$

where NSB is net social benefits, B is benefits and C is costs. Time is readily introduced, but for simplicity we ignore it, and the associated issue of discounting, here. Note, however, that the time/discounting problem is also common to all decision rules.

If some benefits or costs cannot be measured in money terms, then the CBA rule can be modified to an "implicit price rule". Suppose, for example, that it was thought impossible to put money values on health losses arising from the policy. Then the basic requirement is rewritten:

$$NSB = (B - C - H) > O$$

where H is now health costs not measured in money terms. If B and C are measured in money terms then B – C can be expressed as a money total, say \$A. The rule is then:

$$NSB = (\$A - H) > 0, \text{ or simply, } \$A > H.$$

Approached in this way, then, we know that the policy is worthwhile if and only if it is judged (by the decision-maker) that the net money benefits are worth

more than the non-monetised health costs. Incidentally, if H is a number of lives lost, or days of illness, acceptance of the policy will imply that the decision-maker values a life or a day's ill health at less than \$A/H. Rejection of the policy will imply a value at greater than \$A/H. We might therefore present exactly that implication to the decision-maker to assist in the decision process.

CBA does not therefore require that all costs and benefits be measured in money units. But it is clear that benefit measurement is a necessary part of CBA.

2.3. COST-EFFECTIVENESS ANALYSIS

In CEA benefits are not measured in money units, but costs are. We thus have no formal rule for deciding whether a policy is desirable or not. The most that can be done is to present the information on costs and effectiveness. Certain rules will emerge if some prior decisions about policy have been made. For example, it may have been decided to spend \$A on saving lives by improved health screening. If there are several techniques for achieving that screening, the one with the highest value of H/A (or the lowest value of A/H) is to be preferred. Such decisions are very common and it therefore follows that CEA has a significant role to play in real-world decision-making.

What CEA does not tell us is whether the prior policy decision – to invest money in health screening in this case – is worthwhile or not. However, if there is a political decision already made, CEA is an important procedure for ensuring the rational use of limited resources. Moreover, it may overcome resistance by decision-makers to the idea of money valuations of benefits. It is important to note, however, that once they make the decision, for or against, then they have implied a money value, as demonstrated above. CEA is thus seen to be a variant of CBA. To regard it as somehow "superior" or "inferior" is to mistake its relationship with CBA: it comes into use whenever the monetary valuation of benefits (or costs) is thought to be improper or illicit at the stage of the analysis, but when it is logically implied at the stage of decision-making.

2.4. MULTI-CRITERIA ANALYSIS (MULTIPLE OBJECTIVE PROGRAMMING)

CEA becomes complex when the benefits of policy are several and each is expressed in its own units of measurement. Instead of a measure such as H/A in the above example, we might have several "outputs" arising from a policy. They cannot be added together directly because they have no common unit (which would be money in the case of CBA). The requirement must therefore be to place some weighting factor on the individual "outputs". If, for example, reduced accidents were more important than gains in scenic beauty then they will attract a higher importance weight. The various benefits may then be summed in their weighted form. For example, if benefits are health (H), scenic beauty (S) and savings in travel time (T), and each has an importance weight h, s and t respectively, then the overall benefit is B' where:

$$B' = hH + sS + tT$$

Note that the procedure is exactly analogous to the CBA model. The weights h, s and t are in fact "prices" reflecting the relative importance of each of the objectives, but they may be derived in any number of ways – by asking experts, by asking individuals, by asking the decision-maker. The other observation is that the resulting measure B', cannot now be related to costs other than through a cost-effectiveness index B'/C. All the comments on CEA are thus applicable to this approach. We have simplified a good deal, and multi-criteria analysis has become a complex process. Its essential features follow this analysis, however. Yet, multi-criteria analysis does show clearly the multiple objectives that decision-makers generally do have, and if the importance weights can be derived, it enables diverse objectives to be integrated. Compared to CBA, then, the fundamental difference lies in the recognition that economic efficiency frequently is not the sole objective of policy.

2.5. RISK-BENEFIT ANALYSIS

Many policies involve risky events – damage from nuclear power accidents, health risks from chemicals in the environment and so on. The application of decision rules to such areas has led to the emergence of "risk-benefit analysis". Instead of asking about the costs and benefits of a policy consider the costs and benefits of undertaking no action to reduce, say, chemicals in drinking water. The risks of such a policy are the number of cancers arising from the chemicals. The benefits of "no action" are the avoided resource costs of removing the chemicals. We can therefore compare the risks with benefits to give us "risk-benefit analysis" (RBA). Note that, expressed in this way, RBA is nothing more than CBA but in the context of risky events. In CBA a cost is a foregone benefit and a benefit is a foregone cost. RBA simply takes this essential relationship and declares the cancer deaths to be the cost and the foregone resource costs to be the benefits. To see the formal equivalence of CBA and RBA consider the case of nuclear power where the benefit is the value of the electricity produced and the costs are the resource costs and the hazards to human health from a probabilistic accident and form routine emissions of radioactivity. Once again, this fits the CBA framework, but some of the costs are expressed in probabilistic form.

RBA does however focus attention on one problem. Suppose the probability of a nuclear accident is very small, say 1 in a million. The cost of such an accident if it occurred could however be very large indeed. Imagine it amounts to 1 million lives lost or subject to serious health damage. What is the appropriate measure of cost? It must surely be very large indeed because few of us could contemplate an accident involving 1 million people dead or seriously harmed. Yet if we multiply the probability by the "event" we get an *expected value* of

$$1 \times 10^{-6} \times 10^{6} = 1$$

The expected value of lives lost from the accident becomes 1. The problems associated with using expected values are explored in more detail in decision analysis. As we shall see, however, the findings of decision analysis are in no way inconsistent with any other decision rules. Indeed, decision analysis has long been integrated into CBA.

2.6. DECISION ANALYSIS

Decision analysis has developed largely in the context of uncertainty about the outcomes from given actions, or "strategies". The basic idea is that outcomes will not be known with certainty. At best it may be possible to allocate probabilities to benefits or costs. At worst, a range of benefits and costs can be established but it will not be possible to place probabilities on their occurrence. Decision theory also observes that actions and strategies can be taken at several points in the decision process. The decision to invest or not to invest, for example, is the first "node" of the decision process. The decision to invest, however, may then be followed by a second "layer" of decisions, for example whether to invest in a particular area, or in differing financial amounts and so on. All of this is consistent with the other decision rules which would typically regard combinations of different decisions as "different" projects between which the decision rules should choose.

Decision theory proceeds by constructing a "payoff matrix" in which the various outcomes from the different choices are depicted. Such a matrix is shown below for an hypothetical investment:

State of nature	Action	
	Not invest	Invest
Good	100	80
Bad	20	60

The investment decision faces uncertainty in the "state of nature", which could literally be the weather, world price trends or whatever is out of the control of the investing agency. If nature is kind, the payoff (say in crop yields per acre) will be 100 without undertaking any investment (in, say, measures to protect crops against drought or flood). But if nature is unkind, the zero investment policy could result in net yields of only 20. By investing, on the other hand, net yields can be obtained in the range 60-80. Note that net yield is lower in the "good" state of nature case because the payoffs are measured net of the investment cost. Indeed, the payoffs in the matrix can be thought of as net monetary benefits (profit, social profit etc.).

Before proceeding, note that benefit estimation has entered quite explicitly into decision theory. The payoffs are the monetary net benefits of the strategies under different states of nature. We could leave the problem here and observe only that which strategy is chosen will depend on the subjective attitude of the investor. An optimist, for example, might go for no investment in the hope that nature will be kind (a "maximax" policy), whereas a cautious person might go for the investment policy to maximise the minimum payoff (60 in this case: a "maximin" policy). There are no rules for choosing between the different strategies. What is important is to recognise that decision theory has so far done nothing that is not done in any of the other decision rules. This is not because it is inferior or redundant: it simply reflects the fact that at the very early stages of development of cost-benefit and cost-effectiveness rules, decision theory was quite explicitly incorporated into the analysis. It is a misconception to suppose that the approaches "compete" with each other.

However, there is one further stage in decision theory that matters. The payoff matrix above could be converted into a single indicator of net benefit if we agreed on the expected value approach and if probabilities could be placed on the outcomes. For example, if we knew that the "good" state of nature had a probability of 0.6 and that of "bad" 0.4, then the expected value of net social benefits from not undertaking the investment would be:

$$(0.6 \times 100) + (0.4 \times 20) = 65$$

This can be compared to the expected value of the benefits from undertaking the investment which would be:

$$(0.6 \times 80) + (0.4 \times 60) = 72$$

On the expected value criterion the investment is worthwhile.

However, we observed that the idea of taking an "expected value" may not be appropriate if the worst event is particularly unattractive. Consider a different payoff matrix:

State of nature	Action	
	Not invest	Invest
Good	100	50
Bad	0	40

Assume probabilities are known and are the same as before. But this time the bad state of nature results in zero net return if no investment is undertaken: the zero can be thought of as financial ruin, for example. The expected value criterion will, however, result in no investment taking place, the respective expected values being 60 and 54. It would be an optimist indeed who would undertake such a choice.

It is to decision theory that we owe the idea of transforming the problem into one of "expected utilities" rather than expected values. Essentially what happens is that we look at the investor's attitude to risk taking and, assuming he is risk-averse, we attach a high (negative) weight to very adverse circumstances. The choice is then between the value of the expected utility under the two strategies. (If the investor is risk-neutral he will regard equal increments of expected value of net benefits as giving rise to equal utility – his utility function is linear. Risk-averse individuals, however, have non-linear functions where increments of net benefit have fewer and fewer associated increments in utility the higher those benefits are. Similarly, if catastrophes are considered as such they will have large disutility values attached to them.) What decision theory tells us, then, is that in the "normal" case of risk aversion we should expect to weight the net benefits by some index or measure of risk aversion.

This additional feature of decision theory is important, even though decision theory offers us no non-arbitrary way of assigning the utility weights. Again, however, we should observe that decision theory is not in conflict with the other decision rules since any one of them can be adapted to incorporate such weights. Indeed, since the utility function concept is another way of talking about individuals' preferences we would expect the expected utility approach to be reflected in CBA.

2.7. ENVIRONMENTAL IMPACT ASSESSMENT

The practice of EIA varies but it typically requires the identification and measurement of the impacts of any action where those impacts may be adverse or beneficial.

Table 4. **Comparison of decision-aiding techniques**

Conceptual basis/method	Description	Advantages	Disadvantages	Additional references
1. Benefit-cost analysis	Evaluates policies based on a quantification of net benefits (benefits-costs) associated with them.	Considers the value (in terms of what individuals will pay) and costs of actions; translates outcomes into commensurate terms; consistent with judging by efficiency implications.	No direct consideration of distribution of benefits and costs; significant informational requirements; tends to omit outputs whose effects cannot be quantified; tends to lead to maintenance of *status quo*; contingent on existing distribution of income and wealth.	Pearce and Nash (1981)
2. Cost effectiveness analysis	Selects policy that will minimize costs of realizing the policy goal or objectives.	No need to know the benefits; focus is on information often more readily available; provides implicit values of the objective (e.g. marginal cost of increasing by one unit).	No consideration given to relative importance of outputs; degree to which all costs considered will be important to judgments as to "best" approach; how to treat social costs resulting from side effects.	Pearce and Nash (1981)
3. Multiple criteria analysis	Uses of mathematical programming techniques to select projects based on objective functions including weighted goals of decision maker, with explicit consideration of constraints to action and costs.	Offers consistent basis for making all project or regulatory decisions; fully reflects goals and constraints incorporated in model; allows quantification of implicit costs of constraints; permits prioritizing of projects.	Results only as good as inputs to model; unrealistic (1978) characterization of decision process; must supply the weight to be assigned to goals; large information needs for quantification.	Cohon (1978) Zeleny (1982)
4. Risk-benefit analysis	Evaluates benefits associated with a policy in comparison with its risks.	Framework is left vague for flexibility; intended to permit consideration of all risks, benefits and costs; not an automatic decision rule.	Too vague; factors considered to be commensurate are not.	Fischoff *et al.* (1981)
5. Decision analysis	Step-by-step analysis consequences of choices under uncertainty.	Allows various objectives to be used; makes choices explicit. Explicit recognition of uncertainty.	Objectives not always clear; no clear mechanism for assigning weights.	Norton (1984)
6. Environmental impact assessment	Detailed statements of an action's impacts, adverse effects, alternatives; requires a balancing of economic and environmental benefits and costs.	Explicitly requires consideration of environmental effects; ability to monetise does not preempt numeration of all benefits and costs of an action.	Difficult to integrate descriptive analyses of intangible effects with monetary benefits and costs; no clear criteria for using information in decision.	Andrews (1984)

Source: Adapted from Smith (1986). Decision analysis added.

As its name implies, it pays particular attention to the environmental consequences of a policy or action. Typically, alternatives to the policy are also shown. Monetisation may also be included. Indeed, some EIAs encompass a CBA within their wider terms of reference. The objective which determines the listing of gains and losses is often unclear, risking double-counting. Moreover, no aggregation rule need be applied so that decisions are made on the basis of inspecting the matrix of impacts. Like MCA, however, EIA allows for objectives other than economic efficiency to be explicitly recognised.

2.8. CONCLUSION

Much of the "debate" over decision rules is misplaced. The rules do not so much compete with each other as reflect different practical contexts. Risk and uncertainty are integrated into CBA and CEA rules. But which procedure is used tends to be determined by the practical problems of monetary benefit estimation. This is the fundamental reason for the choice of one procedure rather than another. Table 4, adapted from Smith (1986), summarises the salient features of the procedures discussed here.

Chapter 3

TOTAL ECONOMIC VALUE

3.1. INTRODUCTION

In this Chapter we briefly investigate the concept of "total economic value" (TEV). This concept is of central importance in valuing natural environments (and man-made environments) since it provides a perspective on various kinds of benefits that accrue from environmental preservation and improvement. The essential idea is that the benefits are of two basic types: user benefits and intrinsic benefits. Typically, past studies have only concentrated on the former which relate to the use to which environments and natural products are put. Intrinsic benefits, on the other hand, cover values that are placed on natural environments, wildlife, etc. but which are unassociated with any specific use. There is a debate about just what intrinsic benefits actually comprise.

3.2. USER BENEFITS

User benefits comprise consumptive and non-consumptive values. The consumptive value of wildlife, for example, would be the benefits secured by a hunter. The non-consumptive value would be the benefit received by those who like the view and appreciate wildlife. In addition to these values, we have the value placed on natural assets and environments by those who may not wish to make a direct consumptive or non-consumptive use now, but would like to preserve the option of such an act later on. The benefit of knowing the asset will be there when the option is exercised clearly has a monetary value – people should be willing to pay something to preserve the supply of the asset, provided they are certain of their continued preference for it. This type of benefit is known as option value. It so happens that if the individual in question is not certain that he will continue to have preference for the asset then option value can be negative. A proof of this is due to Bishop (1982) and is given in Annex 1. The more familiar case, in which the uncertainty is about the supply of rather than the demand for the asset, will tend to result in an option value being positive. Either way, option value operates like an adjustment to the consumer surplus measure of user benefit. The adjustment arises from uncertainty about either demand or supply, or both. Thus, whether option value is positive or negative, it needs to be added or taken away from the other component of user value to obtain the total user benefit (TUB). That is, we can write:

Total User Benefit = Consumer Surplus +
(–) Option Value

Total user benefit is referred to as option price in the literature. (Note that we have allocated option values to use values, whereas many writers regard option value as a "non-use value". But its motivation is explicitly that of opting to make use of the environmental good in question. Note also that the motive for use value is essentially selfish.)

3.3. INTRINSIC BENEFITS

Many people derive benefit from environmental assets through reading about them, seeing television pictures, listening to talks about them. This "indirect use" of the environment is of some importance and it seems clear that the assets in question have a value because of this indirect or "vicarious" use. It is not clear if such values are part of user benefits or belong as non-use or intrinsic values. We simply note that they are positive.

There are also altruistic motives for preserving environmental assets. The literature remains unclear about the terminology to be used with respect to these motives, but it seems fair to say that what are called *existence values* largely arise from these altruistic motives. Basically, people appear to value some environmental assets – notably wildlife and natural habitats, but also works of art, historic buildings and so on – even though they themselves never expect to see them. The altruism involved can be directed at children, grandchildren and future generations. There may be a simple desire to preserve the asset for the benefit of future generations.

Such altruism is designated the *bequest motive*. The altruism may also be directed at non-human populations. This is more complex and speculative, but many people do have feelings of "stewardship" on behalf of non-human populations because of their general inability to defend themselves in the race for survival with mankind. Evident willingness to pay to preserve environments that will knowingly never be seen by the individual expressing the value is consistent with this motive. The individual effectively values "for" the threatened species. But existence values also appear to be significant for non-living things as well, for example a fine landscape view. In this case altruism does not seem the right word since it is not clear what the object of altruism is.

This brief discussion suggests that to total user benefits we must add total non-user benefits, or intrinsic benefits, where:

Total Intrinsic Benefits =
Existence Value for Future People +
Existence Value of Other Species

Overall, the study of these various types of motivation is still to be developed. It is sufficiently advanced for us

to acknowledge, however, that existence unrelated to user benefits has a value in itself.

When we add total user benefits and total non-user benefits, we obtain total economic value (TEV).

Total Economic Value = Total User Benefit +
Total Intrinsic Benefits

There are other motives, e.g. in preserving natural assets for research, but one would expect these to be subsumed under option value. Some writers include a concept of "quasi-option value" which, in the context of irreversible environmental losses, relates to the value of extra information as the decision to destroy the asset is postponed. But by and large it seems right to subsume this under option value which in turn, as we have seen, becomes an adjustment to use value because of uncertainty about supply or demand.

The concept of TEV is much broader than traditional benefit evaluation approaches. Moreover, there is evidence that the existence value component may be substantial, perhaps dwarfing the use values and especially so where the object of valuation is unique and hence non-reproducible. We shall see some of the results in Chapter 4.

DIRECT VALUATION TECHNIQUES

4.1. INTRODUCTION

The approaches to the economic measurement of environmental benefits have been broadly classified as direct and indirect techniques. The former considers environmental gains – an improved scenic view, better levels of air quality or water quality, etc. – and seeks directly to measure the money value of those gains. This may be done, as indicated in Chapter 1, by looking for a surrogate market or by experimental techniques. The surrogate market approach looks for a market in which goods or factors of production (especially labour services) are bought and sold, and observes that environmental benefits or costs are frequently attributes of those goods or factors. Thus, a fine view or the level of air quality is an attribute or feature of a house, risky environments may be features of certain jobs, and so on. The experimental approach simulates a market by placing respondents in a position in which they can express their hypothetical valuations of real improvements in specific environments. In this second case, the aim is to make the hypothetical valuations as real as possible.

In this Chapter both techniques are illustrated. The "hedonic price" approach applied to the residential housing and labour markets illustrates the surrogate market technique, as does the travel cost approach, where the demand for environmental, particularly recreational, facilities, is valued through an examination of the costs people incur to enjoy them. The "contingent valuation" method illustrates the experimental market approach.

4.2. HEDONIC PROPERTY PRICES

i) The Hedonic Technique

Economists have long recognised that the value of a piece of land is related to the stream of benefits to be derived from that land. Agricultural output and shelter are the most obvious benefits, but access to the workplace, to commercial amenities and to environmental facilities such as parks, and the environmental quality of the neighbourhood are also important benefits which accrue to the person who has the right to use a particular piece of land. The property value approaches to the measurement of benefit estimation are based on this simple underlying assumption, and the most common of them is called the hedonic price approach. Given that different locations have different environmental attributes, there will be differences in property values. With the use of appropriate statistical techniques the hedonic approach attempts to a) *identify* how much of a property value differential is due to a particular environmental difference between properties and b) *infer* how much people are willing to pay for an improvement in the environmental quality and what the social value of the improvement is. Both the identification and the inference activities involve a number of issues which are discussed in some detail below.

The identification of a property price effect due to a difference in pollution levels is usually done by means of a multiple regression technique in which data are taken either on a small number of similar residential properties over a period of years (time series), or on a large number of diverse properties at a point in time (cross section), or on both (pooled data). In practice almost all property value studies have used cross section data, as controlling for other influences over time is much more difficult.

It is well known that differences in residential property values can arise from many sources; these include the amount and quality of accommodation available, the accessibility of the central business district, the level and quality of local public facilities, the level of property taxes; and the environmental characteristics of the neighbourhood, such as the levels of air pollution, traffic and aircraft noise, and access to parks and water facilities. In order to pick up the effects of any of these variables on the value of a property, they *all* have to be included in the analysis. Hence such studies usually involve a number of *property*-describing variables, a number of *neighbourhood* variables, a number of *accessibility* variables and finally the *environmental* variables of interest. If any variable that is relevant is *excluded* from the analysis then the estimated effects on property value of the included variables could be biased. Whether the bias is upward or downward will depend on how the included and excluded variables relate to each other and to the value of the property.

On the other hand if an irrelevant variable is included in the analysis, then no such systematic bias results, although the estimates of the effects of the included variables are rendered somewhat less reliable. This would suggest then that we include as many variables as possible. However, doing so creates another difficulty. Typically many of the variables of interest are very closely correlated. For example, good accessibility to the town centre is often closely related to some measures of air pollution, and one measure of air pollution, such as total suspended particulate matter, is very closely correlated to another measure, such as levels of nitrogen dioxide. What this means is that the data available to us are not rich enough to separate out the effects of these variables. Hence many studies often include only one measure of air pollution and use it to pick up the effects of all forms of air pollution on property values, or use a *proxy* variable such as income to measure the impact of many socio-economic variables on property values. Such procedures are approximate but often necessary. The sensitivity of the estimated coefficients to the selection of the independent variables, to measurement error in these variables and to the estimation procedures can be evaluated using statistical tests as proposed by Klepper and Leamer (1984). Such tests have not generally been applied to hedonic price studies, but the little evidence that is available indicates considerable sensitivity of the hedonic coefficients to the factors mentioned above.

Another issue of importance in the estimation of hedonic price equations is the choice of the functional form used to relate the dependent variable (house prices or property rents) to the explanatory variables listed above. Most studies find that a linear relationship is unsatisfactory and so end up using some non-linear relationship. However, the precise form used can have a significant impact both on the estimated impact of pollution on property values and on the inferred value of the benefits to be derived from an improvement in the environment. The use of statistical criteria in evaluating functional forms is discussed in Halvorsen and Polla-kowski (1981). Although these criteria are helpful, they are not always conclusive and so an element of judgment on the part of the researcher is quite likely to arise.

Other problems at this stage of the hedonic price exercise relate to the measurement of the variables. First there is the measurement of the dependent variable. For this, either data on house prices or house rents can be used. In general house prices are more frequently used than house rents; partly because more property is owner-occupied in the countries and areas where much of the work has been done and partly because rents are often found to perform less well in such exercises than house prices. Such price data can be based on actual sales (which have been used in some of the recent studies), or on professional valuations of the properties. Although such estimates are bound to have some errors in them, tests such as those done by Nelson (1978a) show that the errors are not systematic or too significant, at least in the United States. American hedonic price studies have also taken, as the variable to be explained, the average or median property price over a census tract. Such data have the advantage of "ironing out" random variations in prices and, as long as the tracts are relatively homogeneous, they should prove to be satisfactory working variables. However, it is preferable to use actual sales price data where possible and indeed the more recent studies in this area have been doing that.

The other crucial variable to be measured is of course the level of pollution. In air pollution studies, suspended particulates are the most common, and oxidants and measures of sulphate pollution have also been found to be a significant influence on property values. One difficulty with such measures is that they are frequently highly correlated and so only one or at the most two can be included. Another is that the appropriate measure is not clear. Should it be the annual average, or the geometric mean? Should one take account of the variation in concentrations? For noise nuisance there are alternative measures of noise levels that stress different aspects of the noise problem. In principle the issue here is clear: try all measures and choose the best. In practice, however, the choice is not easy to make on statistical grounds and one is left with an area of uncertainty. A third question that has to be resolved is the choice of the minimum level of pollution. A minimum level is introduced because pollution levels below that do not have a noticeable effect on human beings and therefore do not affect property values. However, the choice of this minimum value has a significant effect on the cost of environmental pollution that is inferred from the study. In principle this level should also be chosen to obtain the best "fit" to the data but in practice the statistical procedures cannot discriminate between small changes in this parameter.

Overall we take the view that environmental pollution in the form of air-pollution, noise nuisance and water quality deterioration have significant effects on the property values on which they impinge. The over-whelming evidence of the empirical studies supports this conclusion. The accuracy with which we can quantify such effects is, however, much more debatable. There are many reasons for thinking the numbers can only be orders of magnitude, and we have alluded to the main ones in our discussion above. It is also our opinion that this matter of fuzziness is not one that will be resolved by better measurement or better statistical techniques: it is inherent to the problem being considered.

ii)   Inferring the Demand for Environmental Quality

The estimation of a relationship between property values and environmental quality indicators is only the first half of the hedonic price approach. Such an estimated relationship is used to infer the individual and social costs of environmental pollution (or the benefit of reducing such pollution). It is to this question of inference that we now turn.

Figure 3 shows a typical relationship between pollution and property values that might be uncovered by the hedonic price techniques. It shows that as the pollution level decreases, so property values rise, but at a declining rate. Figure 4 plots the slope of the relationship in Figure 3 against the level of pollution. This is shown as AB. Hence it gives, for each level of pollution, the amount by which property values would fall if pollution levels were to be increased by a small amount.

If we are to obtain an estimate of the demand for environmental quality we would like to know how much households are willing to pay for given levels of environmental quality. In Figure 4 consider an individual or household who is living in an environment with an ambient pollution level P^0. It is assumed in the hedonic methodology that this choice has been arrived at in a rational manner. That is to say the household concerned has weighed the benefits of living in alternative locations against the costs and on balance has chosen location P^0. To arrive at this decision it must have concluded that the extra payment required in higher property prices for an improvement in the environment from a pollution level slightly higher than P^0, to P^0 is just equal to the benefits of that improvement. Hence we can define the amount W^0 as that household's willingness to pay for the last unit of environmental quality. But such a willingness to pay is a point on the household's demand curve, and other such points are indicated by the broken line CD through E^0.

What this shows us is that the estimated hedonic price relationship can be used to obtain *a point* on each household's demand curve, and that the slope of the estimated relationship is a locus of points on the demand curves of many different households. If all such households were identical in every respect then the derived curve AB in Figure 4 would also be the demand curve for environmental quality. Each household's willingness to pay for a small improvement at every level of pollution P must also be every other household's willingness to pay if they are all identical, and the locus of willingness to pay points defines the demand curve. In general, however, households will differ in income and preference for environmental quality. When that is the case the hedonic approach as outlined so far only gives us partial information on the demand structure. What is now required is to see how this marginal willingness to pay varies with *household income* and other *household characteristics*. This involves a further statistical exercise which would then estimate the (inverse) demand function for environmental quality. At this second stage there is some debate as to how much we need to control for supply influences. The points observed on the curve

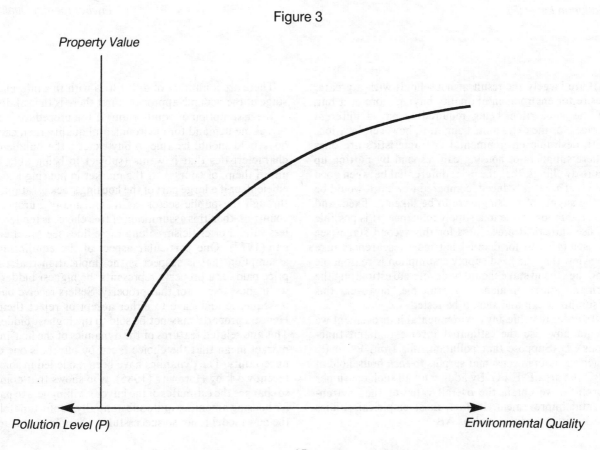

Figure 3

Property Value

Pollution Level (P)

Environmental Quality

27

Figure 4

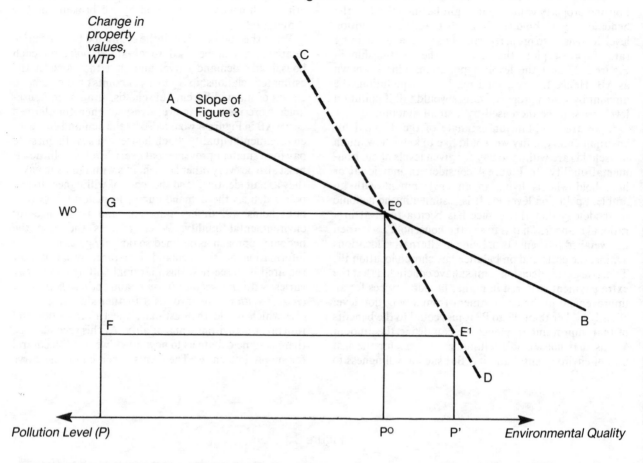

AB are largely the result of households with a greater desire for environmental quality buying more of it but, at the same time, being required to pay a different "price" for the extra units bought. If, however, locations with desirable environmental characteristics are ones where suppliers of housing can respond by putting up more dwellings, then the price differential between good and bad areas is reduced, compared to what it would be if the supply of housing were to be taken as fixed, and this reduction is due to a supply influence. It is possible to use statistical procedures for this second stage [see Nelson (1978b) for details] but most researchers take the view that the fixed supply assumption is reasonable and the second stage should be devoted to estimating the demand function alone. In principle, however, this assumption can and should be tested.

In order to value any environmental improvement we would now use the estimated inverse demand functions CD. Suppose that pollution falls from P^0 to P'. Then the gain in consumer surplus to *each* household at P^0 is the area E^0E^1FG. By adding up all such consumer surpluses we obtain the overall value of the environmental improvement. In fact, most empirical studies work with schedules such as AB.

There are a number of difficulties with this inference stage of the hedonic approach. First there is the validity of the assumption of equilibrium. If the procedure is to reveal the demand for environmental quality then each household should be able to buy exactly the bundle of characteristics that it wants (subject to being able to afford them, of course). If the market in housing is not efficient, or if a large part of the housing stock is rationed through the public sector, as it is in many European countries, then this assumption of free choice is rendered less valid. For criticisms along these lines see MacLennan (1977). One particular aspect of the equilibrium assumption that is suspect is the implication that the price paid for a property represents the highest bidder's willingness to pay for that property. Sellers receive bids in sequence and have to either accept or reject them. Hence a property may not be sold to the highest bidder. This and related features of the dynamics of the housing market mean that the choice faced by buyers is one of uncertainty. The dynamics have been modelled in some recent work by Horowitz (1985), who shows that doing so changes the estimates of the buyer's willingness to pay for housing amenities quite substantially. Unfortunately the new model is not so successful in obtaining satisfactory results on air pollution indices, but seems to perform better on other indicators. This work needs to be developed further before some firm conclusions can be drawn on its implications for our current hedonic estimates of the willingness to pay for environmental quality.

A second problem that one faces is related to the issue of market segmentation. Even if the housing market works well in each area, mobility between areas of a conurbation may be severely restricted. In that case the demand for environmental quality should be separately assessed for each area and pooling the data could result in biased estimates. This point is discussed in some detail by Freeman (1979a). Third, a complication arises because there are more ways of mitigating the effects of environmental pollution than by moving location. With air pollution one can install filters so that at least inside the house the quality of air is improved, and with noise nuisance there is the prospect of double glazing and other noise reduction measures. Such "averting behaviour" has been discussed by Freeman (1979b). He finds that it has implications for the estimation of benefits from property value data. If averting behaviour involves physical changes to the house then it will enhance the value of the house but such increases in value are a cost attributable to the environmental pollution. Hence such attributes of housing should be included in the hedonic exercise but frequently they are not for lack of data. On the other hand if averting behaviour is necessary but not a part of the physical features of the house, then it reduces the value of the property and need not be measured separately.

The question of exactly what the willingness to pay curve measures raises other related issues. Of course households can only be expected to pay for environmental quality to the extent that they perceive the lack of it to be harmful or unpleasant to them. Lack of knowledge of the health risks of certain forms of environmental pollution will inevitably lead to an underestimate of the social benefit of reducing such pollution. Nor is it easy to overcome such an underestimate by tagging on to the hedonic price estimate a figure for the health costs, or any other costs of pollution, as derived by another of the methods discussed in this survey. This could involve double counting, because at least part of the health benefits or property damage benefits are perceived and capitalized in property values. The only environmental benefits that can be properly added to those measured by the hedonic technique are those that are not related to residential choice. For example, pollution at the place of work or the general pollution level in a whole town cannot be overcome by residential choice. Under certain conditions the monetary valuation of such pollution can be derived from wage data (see Section 4.3) and added to the hedonic price valuations.

Finally, care must be taken when doing hedonic price studies in going from annual benefits to present value benefits. As stated earlier, most hedonic price studies

look at the impact on property prices of environmental attributes. Such prices of course capitalize present and future benefits to be derived from the environment. In order to get the annual benefits from the price data, we need to know what the annual return on the property is, as well as what rates of taxation apply both to the property and to the individual. For example the higher the rate of property tax, the greater the annual benefit that is associated with a given property value. This is because the discounted present value of rents net of taxes has to equal the property value. So adjustment has to be made for such taxes (Freeman 1979b). In addition, however, we need to know what individual expectations of future pollution levels are. If such levels are expected to decrease everywhere then property prices will be higher than they would be if they were expected to remain constant. Hence interpreting the hedonic price as the price of the current level of the attribute is likely to lead to an overestimate of willingness to pay. In general, however, the biases resulting from a failure to take account of expectations are quite complex and have been examined in some detail in Abelson and Markandya (1985).

iii) Empirical Results

In Tables 5, 6 and 7 we summarise the main findings of hedonic price studies on aircraft noise, traffic noise and air pollution respectively. The results in the North American and United Kingdom studies refer to a "standardised value" house – one costing about (US) $28 000 in 1970 or about $71 000 in 1986. The reason for this standardization is to eliminate the possibility that higher priced properties may have a greater percentage depreciation than lower priced ones – a finding which occasionally comes up in the research.

Table 5 has two noise measures, both of which attempt to pick up the impact of aircraft noise on human hearing and discomfort. The results obtained here are fairly consistent and suggest that a unit reduction of NEF would appreciate properties by about 0.7 per cent while a unit reduction of NNI would appreciate them by about 0.5 per cent. The maximum tolerable noise level is around 55 NEF; consequently aircraft noise can result in property depreciation of as much as 38 per cent if depreciation continued at a constant rate until the index reached zero. In fact the rate of depreciation appears to fall with the level of noise and is zero after a level of 25-35 NEF is reached. This "zero" point is important in determining the overall cost of the noise in terms of property depreciation but, unfortunately, as we pointed out earlier, its value is not well determined by the estimating equation. Table 6 measures traffic noise in Leq units, which express fluctuating noise levels over a given time interval in terms of an equivalent constant sound pressure. This Table is also suggestive of fairly consistent results, and one can reasonably accept that the numbers between different areas and different

Table 5. **The impact of aircraft noise on house prices**
per cent of house price

Location	Impact of one unit change in NEF	Impact of one unit change in NNI
United States		
Los Angeles	–	0.78
Englewood	–	0.78
New-York	1.60-2.00	–
Minneapolis	0.58	–
San Francisco	0.50	–
Boston	0.83	–
Washington DC	1.00	–
Dallas	0.58-0.80	–
Rochester	0.55-0.68	–
United Kingdom		
Heathrow	–	0.25-0.30
Canada		
Toronto	–	0.18-0.60
Edmonton	0.50	–
Australia		
Sydney	0.00-0.40	–
Switzerland		
Basel	–	0.22
Netherlands		
Amsterdam	–	0.35-0.50

NEF and NNI are measures of aircraft noise related to human hearing and discomfort.
Sources: Nelson (1980), Opschoor (1986) and Pommerehne (1986).

studies will vary by as much as they do. The average effect of an increase in traffic noise of one decibel according to this Table is about one half of one per cent. When referring to the "average" figures, it should be borne in mind that, as for aircraft noise, depreciation per unit in noise often increases with the noise level itself.

In Table 7 we report the results of air pollution studies where significant effects of air pollution on property values have been found and where these effects can be expressed irrespective of the units of measurement of pollution or property values (i.e. in percentage terms). As stated earlier, many such studies find it difficult to distinguish between different forms of air pollution because of their strong inter-correlation. In these cases the one pollution measure included inevitably picks up the effects of all forms of air pollution with which it is strongly correlated. The results in Table 7 suggest that a one per cent increase in sulphation levels will result in falls in property values between 0.06 and 0.12 per cent. A similar increase in particulates lowers property values by between 0.05 and 0.14 per cent. Where the pollution variable is picking up more than one measure of air pollution, property value falls of between 0.09 and 0.5 per cent are recorded. Again we should note that the fall in property values per unit increase in pollution could vary with the level of pollution.

iv) Conclusion

In conclusion, we would say that the hedonic price technique has been used effectively to show the impact of environmental factors on property values. It is particularly well suited to estimating the costs of air and noise pollution on the residential environment but it works poorly if the form of pollution is one whose effects are unclear to the individuals affected and which cannot be easily measured or quantified. The results obtained for sulphate and particulate air pollution and for road and air traffic noise are broadly consistent across studies, and with those obtained by other techniques. Also there has been considerable improvement over the last ten years or so in the quality of the data used and in the analytical techniques employed. These improvements have resulted in better estimates for the hedonic coefficients but, more importantly, they have resulted in a greater awareness of the accuracy of the estimates. It has now become clear that, even with the best techniques at our disposal, this accuracy remains quite low and that the estimated costs by this technique could be out by a substantial margin in either direction. Although this may sound pessimistic, there are many situations where quantification to even an order-of-magnitude is a useful tool in the formulation of environmental policy. In our opinion the hedonic price method, when applied carefully and in the right situation, is capable of a greater level of accuracy than that.

Table 6. **The impact of traffic noise on house prices**
per cent of house price

Location	Impact of one unit change in L_{eq}
United States	
North Virginia	0.15
Tidewater	0.14
North Springfield	0.18-0.50
Towson	0.54
Washington	0.88
Kingsgate	0.48
North King County	0.30
Spokane	0.08
Chicago	0.65
Canada	
Toronto	1.05
Switzerland	
Basel	1.26

Equivalent continuous sound level (L_{eq}) = a level of constant sound (in dBA) which would have the same sound energy over a given period as the measured fluctuating sound under consideration.
Sources: Fuller details of the studies are given in Nelson (1982) and Pommerehne (1986).

Table 7.   **Impact of air pollution on property values**

City	Year of: a) Property data b) Pollution measure	Pollution	% Fall in property value % Increase in pollution
St-Louis	1960 1963	Sulfation Particulates	0.06-0.10 0.12-0.14
Chicago[1]	1964-67 1964-67	Particulates and sulphation	0.20-0.50
Washington	1970 1967-68	Particulates Oxidants	0.05-0.12 0.01-0.02
Toronto-Hamilton	1961	Sulfation	0.06-0.12
Philadelphia	1960 1969	Sulfation Particulates	0.10 0.12
Pittsburgh[1]	1970 1969	Dustfall and sulphation	0.09-0.15
Los Angeles[1]	1977-78 1977-78	Particulates and oxidants	0.22

1.   In these studies it is clear that part of the elasticity that is estimated is due to the form of pollution that is not included in the analysis, or if included has an insignificant impact. This problem of multicollinearity has been discussed in the text.
Sources: Freeman (1979b), Brookshire *et al.* (1982)

4.3.   WAGE RISK STUDIES AND THE VALUE OF LIFE

i)   Willingness to Pay and Willingness to Accept Changes in the Risk of Death

Since one effect of pollution is to damage human health, the benefits of environmental improvement are likely to include improvements in health. These will consist of reduced morbidity and reduced mortality. In the case of mortality, then, benefit estimation requires that we place a money value on changes in risk of death. The literature on this subject is often referred to as the "Value of Life" literature, and there is considerable debate on whether it makes logical sense to speak of a money value of human life (see, for example, the debate between Broome and others in the *Journal of Public Economics*, Broome (1978), Buchanan and Faith (1979), Jones-Lee (1979), Mishan (1981), Ulph (1982). The oddity is easily illustrated if we think of an event that would cause certain death to a known individual (ourselves, say). Applying willingness to pay and willingness to accept principles will tend to result in odd outcomes. We would obviously be willing to pay everything we have and could borrow (save a little for subsistence) to forego the certainty of death and we would not be willing to accept anything to have to face that certainty, since we will not be alive to receive the compensation.

The difficulty with this characterisation of the problem is that environmental policies do not deal with the *certain* death of a *known* individual. What they deal with is the "population at risk" such that the probability of death can be reduced from one level to another, say

from 1 in 100 000 to 1 in 200 000. Compare this to a decision to launch a lifeboat to save a lone yachtsman in trouble at sea. In that case the individual is known and the risk from death very high, if not certain. This distinction helps to explain why very large sums are often spent saving single lives in comparison to the sums involved in saving what are, before the event, "statistical lives". Of course, after the event, the "statistical lives" become known lives – named people die from the pollution. It is important to recognise then, that what the economics literature refers to as "the value of life" is the value in this "before the event" sense (the *ex ante* value, as the literature calls it).

Provided this distinction is valid, and some writers do continue to dispute whether it makes any difference to the objections to putting a money value on life, it is possible to utilise our WTP and WTA concepts as follows. Because of a policy of reducing sulphur oxide emissions, suppose that the death rate falls from 1 in 100 000 (written as "1 in 10^5" or "10^{-5}") to 1 in 200 000 (written as "1 in 2.10^5" or 5×10^{-6}). Suppose that the population that benefits from this reduced statistical risk is 2 million and that each one of them is willing to pay \$5 to secure the risk reduction. Then we can write the value of life as VOL where:

$$\text{VOL} = \$5/(0.00005) = \$1 \text{ million.}$$

Equivalently, the number of deaths was previously $2\,000\,000 \times 10^{-5} = 20$. It falls to $2\,000\,000 \times 5 \times 10^{-6} = 10$, so that 10 lives have been saved. Each individual at risk is prepared to pay \$5 to save these 10 lives (the life that may be saved may be their own), so that we can write:

$$\text{VOL} = \$5 \times 2,000,000/10 = \$1 \text{ million.}$$

31

This is the basic rationale of the WTP approach. Note that the lives saved are "anonymous" before the event (i.e. before the policy decision) and that the WTP is for a reduction in the probability of death. This latter point is sometimes obscured when the figures are presented in a "Value of Life" form and it has been suggested [Viscusi (1986)] that perhaps this is not the best way of presenting and comparing the WTPs in different studies.

In line with the earlier discussion of WTP and WTA, the procedure should work in reverse. That is, it should be possible to argue that compensation will be accepted for an increased probability of death. For small changes in probability, economic theory would suggest that WTA for an increased risk and WTP for a reduced risk should not differ very much. As we saw in Chapter 1, however, this "symmetry" appears not to hold for other objects of value. At present we cannot say for certain whether it holds for the value of life, primarily because there are no studies in which it is possible to control for the same population exposed to the same risks and to vary the risks in one direction and then in another. The only approach available for answering this question is the direct questionnaire approach. However, both WTP and WTA can be measured for different populations. Thus, expenditures on safety measures such as car seat belts, fire sprinkler systems, protective clothing, etc. give us a context in which people imply a willingness to pay for reduced probabilities of death or injury. Similarly, if wage rates are, other things being equal, higher in risky occupations than in less risky ones, then there should be some relationship between the "wage risk premium" and the probability of death or injury. This wage risk premium would qualify as a measure of the willingness to accept compensation. Both these contexts then qualify as ones in which money is paid or received for changes in the probability of death or injury. Both are therefore potentially fruitful areas for obtaining the data on which a value of life can be based.

The context we have selected here is the wage risk premium one. By and large this is because it is amenable to fairly sophisticated approaches and because the number of studies that have been carried out are, to some extent, comparable with each other, thus permitting an inspection of the various estimates and the possibility of a "consensus" estimate. After outlining the general literature (the theory is provided in Annex 3 to this study), we discuss in more detail a study for the United Kingdom.

ii) Wage Risk Studies

Wage risk approaches utilise the same basic idea as in the hedonic property price approach (see Chapter 4.2). The wage rate paid for a job reflects forces of supply and demand in the labour market. But what is demanded and supplied is a set of job characteristics or attributes. One of these attributes is safety so that, if the market functions freely, we would expect, other things being equal, that employers will want to see lower wages to compensate for expenditure on higher safety, and employees will want to see higher wages to compensate for higher risk. This establishes the potential for a bargain in such a way that a price for safety will emerge. This price is the "hedonic wage".

It will be apparent that the presence of risk premiums in wages will only come about if the market is fairly free and if the workers actually perceive workplace safety risks. The presence of trade unions is often cited as the main reason why the labour market is unlikely to function freely. Wage premiums may still exist, but they could be influenced by the power of trade unions to bargain wages in risky conditions. A premium would normally exist but it would be hard to argue that it reflected the WTA for increased workplace risk [for a theoretical analysis of the impact of unions on the wage premium, see Dickens (1984)]. The perception of risk presents a whole host of problems. If there is no awareness of risk then the wage premium might not exist and we might wrongly conclude that there is a zero price for the risk. If there is awareness, the problem arises of whether "true" and "perceived" risk coincide. This is a familiar problem in all risk evaluations. The scientific community argues that what matters is some "objective" probability of a fatality, and not what the workforce or the public think the risk is. But if we are concerned with preferences – and this is the underlying rationale for benefit measurement – then what matters is preferences based on perceptions by those at risk. Thus the only admissible problem on perception is whether or not risk is perceived to be present.

The obvious thing to do in these circumstances is to test the theory against empirical evidence on wage rates. One of the earlier sophisticated and careful studies on this subject is that of Marin and Psacharopoulos (1982) for the United Kingdom. We will outline the results of that study.

iii) The Marin-Psacharopoulos Study

The authors (hereafter M-P) looked at data on deaths classified by occupation for the period 1970-72. Initially they consider the "excess death rate" in various occupations, defined as the actual death rate minus the death rate that could be expected for the age and social class of the workers in each occupation. The problem with this measure – which was widely used in wage risk studies – is that the process of ascribing occupations to those who have died is often uncertain. Another problem is that some of the occupations listed are not those in which the individuals contracted the disease from which they die – surface miners for example have a higher death rate than coal-face miners, but only because coal-face miners are transferred to surface jobs when some disease is detected.

For these and other reasons, M-P prefer to use the rate of deaths from an *accident* and to deduct from this the expected death rate applicable to that age and occupation. Instead of an excess death rate, we have an excess death rate due to accidents. Note also that this variable is likely to solve the problem of risk perception. It is unlikely that workers are not aware of the risk of accidents in the workplace. It also fulfils the condition that it is "job specific", whereas deaths in general could be related to some factors that have nothing to do with job risks. Making use of household information combined with the data on risks, M-P estimate an "earnings function" – an equation which relates annual earnings to various factors (attributes) affecting those earnings. The equation they use, in general form, is:

$$\ln(Y) = f(S, Ex, Ex^2, \ln(Weeks), Risk, Union, Occ, Union \times Risk)$$

In this equation ln refers to logarithms – it is very often more convenient to work with the logarithm of a number than with the number itself; S is a measure of the extent of education (which we would expect to influence earnings positively); Ex is years of experience in the labour force; Weeks is the number of weeks worked in the year of the survey; Risk is the death rate measure discussed above; UNION is a measure of the degree of unionisation; OCC is a measure of the desirability of the occupation, and Union×Risk indicates a possible interaction between unionisation and risk.

M-P report various statistical tests of the basic equation. The actual procedure is to use linear multiple regression. Taking accident risks as a whole, they found that there is a negative sign on the coefficient of Union × Risk, which means that unionisation actually weakens the premium pertaining to risk. A theoretical explanation of this has been provided by Dickens (1984). The reason is simply that, bargaining rationally to maximise their workers' interests, unions need not raise wages by more than a competitive market would when risk increases. Indeed it can be shown that under plausible conditions the reverse could be true. However, the coefficient on that variable is statistically insignificant (at the 5 per cent level of significance), so M-P show what happens when it is dropped from the specification. We report their finding for accident rates in general with the Union × Risk variable dropped. The estimated equation is:

$$\ln(Y) = 1.95 + 0.058(S) + 0.046(Ex) \\ -0.0008(Ex^2) + 1.13\ln(Weeks) \\ +0.029(Risk) + 0.002(Union) + 0.008(Occ)$$

Each of the coefficients in this regression is statistically significant. The relevant coefficient for the value of life is the 0.029 on Risk. Because the results are to be expressed in terms of risks of death per 1 000 workers (any standardisation would do, but this is a commonly used one), a sum of £Z required by each worker to compensate for an increased risk of death of 1 in 1 000 translates to 1 000Z for 1 000 workers in all. The value of life is then calculated as $1000[\delta Y/\delta Risk]$ where

δ stands for "change in". Since $\delta Y = Y(\delta \ln(Y))$, the value of life is:

$$1\,000.Y(\delta \ln(Y)\delta Risk)$$

But the term in brackets is the coefficient on Risk in the regression equation, i.e. 0.229. Thus, so long as we know average income, we can calculate the value of life.

In the M-P study the value of life turns out to be £600 000 in 1975 prices for the regression including the Union × Risk term, and £681 000 for the regression excluding this term. M-P go on to disaggregate their findings to different occupational groups. For non-manual workers the value of life is some £2 245 000 in 1985 prices, and £686 000 for manual workers. Taking the weighted average for these two groups, the value of life, in 1985 prices, comes to £1.88 million.

iv) Comparison with Other Studies

M-P compare their estimates with those obtained from United States studies. Rather than convert value of life figures to a common basis, they compare the number of deaths per annum per 1 000 workers. Since their paper, new American studies have appeared so that we are able to present a summary comparison of them in Table 8. Considerable caution, however, needs to be exercised in any such comparison. While they are standardised for risks per annum per 1000 workers, the original units vary significantly and the surveys by M-P and Violette and Chestnut (1983) disagree significantly on the mean risk levels that emerge from the studies by R. Smith (1974) and Viscusi (1978). A further survey

Table 8. **Value of life in occupational risk studies: United States and United Kingdom**

Study	Risk level (annual deaths per annum per 1000 workers)	Best estimate of the value of life (USA=$Mn., UK=£Mn. All in 1982 prices)
United States		
Arnould/Nichols (1983)	1.10	0.64
Dillingham (1979)	0.17	0.40
Olson (1981)	0.10	7.10
Smith, R (1974)	0.10-0.15	7.50
Smith, R (1976)	0.10-0.15	3.30
Smith, V (1982)	0.30	3.50
Thaler/Rosen (1975)	1.10	0.57
Viscusi (1978b)	0.12	2.9-3.9
Viscusi (1981)		7.0-11.0
United Kingdom		
M-P (1982)	0.23	1.64
Veljanovski (1980)	0.05	3.39-4.59
Needleman (1979)	2.21	0.13-0.72

Source: Adapted from Violette and Chestnut (1983) with corrections; Marin and Psacharopolos (1982), Veljanovski (1981), Viscusi (1986).

by Veljanovski (1981) reports risk levels that are consistent with the Violette and Chestnut data.

Table 8 reveals a wide disparity of estimates for the value of life. It is tempting to think that the differences are accounted for by differing risks: that is, the higher the risk, the greater the compensation expected. In fact exactly the opposite appears to be the case. At high levels of risk, the value of life is often less. Compare, for example, the Thaler and Rosen and Arnould and Nichols estimates for the high risk categories with the Olson and Smith studies for much lower risks. The same pattern appears to hold for the much more limited sample of studies for the United Kingdom. One reason for this is the likelihood that high risk industries (notably building and construction) attract less risk-averse work-forces. There is perhaps an element of risk-loving or risk indifference in some of the high risk industries. M-P show that the differences also arise from other factors such as the nature of the risk variable used. Thus Thaler and Rosen use excess death rates not accident deaths, and the latter are more likely to give higher value of life figures. Similarly the studies by Viscusi (1978b) and Smith (1974) concern blue collar workers and values of life for such workers are likely to be significantly higher. M-P conclude that the dominant reason for the difference in estimates in the United States studies arises from the use of the more relevant measure of risk – accident risk – in the higher value studies. In turn this suggests that the figures near the top of the range are more relevant for benefit valuation purposes. It is also indicative that, using an exchange rate of $2 = £1, the M-P figures are towards the top end of the United States range.

Another reason given for a wide variety of results in wage risk studies is that

"the available data may simply be inadequate to support investigations of market performance" [Dickens (1984)].

Dickens reaches this conclusion by estimating several wage risk equations in which the sample is split up between unionised and non-unionised workers. In most specifications of the model he finds a *negative* coefficient on the risk term (measuring the risk of fatal injury) for non-unionised workers, but a positive one for unionised workers. There is no reasonable explanation for this and so one must conclude that, for some categories of workers at least, risk differentials are not compensated for by wage differentials.

An interesting study that gives some support to the figures obtained by M-P is that by Jones-Lee, Hammerton and Philips (1985). They obtain information on the value of the risk of death by using a questionnaire approach (discussed in detail in Section 4.4). Respondents were asked questions about their willingness to pay for changes in risk in a variety of situations, most of which related to the risk of death in road accidents. The responses obtained showed that the value of life in this risk context, if one excluded some outlying and inconsistent responses, ranged from £1.21 million to £2.21 million, with a mean of £1.5 million, all in 1982 prices. This mean is remarkably close to the M-P figure of £1.64 million. The variation in the estimates obtained by Jones-Lee et al. arose from variation in the reduction in risk and the level at which the reduction is applied. They also found that, quite plausibly, the willingness to pay to avoid death depended on how one was assumed to die, and that if one looked at the distribution of the willingness to pay, the means quoted above are considerably above their respective medians (almost 90 per cent higher). Hence the mean value is not quite as representative of willingness to pay for risk reduction as one might think.

v) Inferring the Value of Life in a Pollution Risk Context

Can these values be used to value life in the context of risks of death from pollution? The first problem is that pollution exposure is usually related to low probabilities of death, although these probabilities may affect a large number of people. Thus, typical exposure to radiation is at very low levels and the consequent probability of death is very low. This exposure may be very limited – say, to small groups of workers in nuclear power plants, or local populations in the neighbourhood of such plants. Sulphur oxide pollution, however, can have similar low probabilities of death associated with it, but can relate to very large populations – whole cities, for example. This suggests that the relevant values of life are those relating to low probabilities of death. The empirical literature reviewed here suggests that low probabilities are associated with high values of life. If this is correct, it places a high value on policies which set out to prevent pollution damage rather than remedial policies which deal with the consequences of the event through the health care of the sick. Not only is the policy implication important, but this result contradicts the expectations literature. The theory would suggest that higher values of life are associated with higher risks of death [Rosen (1981)].

The second issue is that the wage risk studies relate to compensation received for increases in risk over some "average" level. The studies of benefits from air pollution tend to operate with the concept of willingness to pay for reductions in pollution. As we noted, if people behave as economic theory predicts the difference between the two measures ought to be small. But there is some uncertainty about this, as we have seen.

The third issue is that the wage risk premium is compensation received for a voluntarily accepted risk. Some risks can be said to be imposed, in which case the compensation required can be many times the amount required for accepting a voluntary risk, perhaps even 100 times more [Litai (1980)]. Exactly what the relationship is between voluntary and involuntary risks, WTA and WTP is uncertain. Table 9 shows a possible typology and suggested approaches. In this table, R refers to the change in risk, so that R 0 is an increase

Table 9.	**Typology for risk contexts**	
	Voluntary	Involuntary
$\Delta R > 0$	WTA(V)	WTA(I)
$\Delta R > 0$	WTP(I)	?

satisfied then some indirect valuation procedure may be necessary. Alternatively, as at least one recent study has shown, it may be possible to use contingent valuation techniques.

in risk. WTA(V) then relates to a wage risk context, or any other context in which people are willing to accept an increase in risk in return for compensation, but a risk they do not have to tolerate if they so choose. WTA(I) refers to a context in which the risk is imposed on the population so that they cannot choose whether to accept it or not. In such contexts the compensation that would make them as well off as before could be orders of magnitude greater than for voluntarily accepted risk, i.e. $WTA(I) > k.WTA(V)$, where $k > 1$. WTP(V) relates to contexts of unusual environmental policy where WTP is positive (if it were zero, the policy would not be implemented). The most uncertain classification is the involuntary risk reduction situation. If people are risk-averse this category would seem self contradictory, but many examples exist, as with the introduction of the compulsory wearing of seat belts in cars.

From this discussion it will be evident that choosing the "right" value of life for pollution contexts is not at all straightforward. At the very least it must take account of the social context in which the policy or risk occurs.

vi) Conclusions

Wage risk studies have improved a great deal in recent years and have become quite sophisticated. The quality of the data that can be gathered for these studies is generally good and so the estimated coefficients for the risk variables are capable of being well determined. However, although in each of the studies we have looked at this is the case, the consistency across the studies is weak and the implied value of life has quite a broad range. Indeed some of the studies have found negative coefficients in the risk variables among non-unionised workers.

In addition we face further difficulties in using these coefficients in the contexts of an increased exposure to pollution. The arguments that have been presented suggest that these costs may be underestimated by the wage risk study method. The magnitude of the error will be less if the probability of mortality in the wage risk study is similar to that of the pollution context in which it is being used, if the groups affected in the two cases are not dissimilar, if the perception of the pollution is realistic, and if the labour market from which the data are drawn is well functioning. In these circumstances the costs of mortality can be usefully measured using the wage risk study method. If these conditions are not

4.4. CONTINGENT VALUATION

i) Aim and Approach of the CVM

The contingent valuation method (CVM) has been applied with increasing frequency to the measurement of environmental policy benefits and damage costs. CVM uses a direct approach – it basically asks people what they are willing to pay for a benefit, and/or what they are willing to receive by way of compensation to tolerate a cost. This process of "asking" may be either through a direct questionnaire/survey, or by experimental techniques in which subjects respond to various stimuli in "laboratory" conditions. What is sought are the personal valuations of the respondent for increases or decreases in the quantity of some good, contingent upon an hypothetical market. Respondents say what they would be willing to pay or willing to accept if a market existed for the good in question. A contingent market is taken to include not just the good itself (an improved view, better water quality, etc.), but also the institutional context in which it would be provided, and the way in which it would be financed.

One major attraction of CVM is that it should, technically, be applicable to all circumstances. This contrasts with, say, house price or travel cost approaches where information may not always be available, or relevant. In short, CVM has two important features:

– It will frequently be the only technique of benefit estimation;
– It should be applicable to most contexts of environmental policy.

The aim of the CVM is to elicit valuations – or "bids" – which are close to those that would be revealed if an actual market existed. The hypothetical market – the questioner, questionnaire and respondent – must therefore be as close as possible to a real market. The respondent must, for example, be familiar with the good in question. If the good is improved scenic visibility, this might be achieved by showing the respondent photographs of the view with and without particular levels of pollution. The respondent must also be familiar with the hypothetical means of payment – say a local tax or direct entry charge – known as the payment *vehicle*.

The questioner suggests the first bid [the "starting point bid (price)"] and the respondent agrees or denies that he/she would be willing to pay it. An iterative procedure follows: the starting point price is increased to see if the respondent would still be willing to pay it, and so on until the respondent declares he/she is not willing to pay the extra increment in the bid. The last accepted bid, then, is the maximum willingness to pay (MWTP). The process works in reverse if the aim is to elicit willingness to accept (WTA): bids are systematically lowered until the respondent's minimum WTA is reached.

Designs of CVM questionnaires vary. Respondents may be given hypothetical budgets to allocate between expenditures, or they may be told about the bids made by other respondents. The variability in the design is useful because it permits some testing of the relevance of including certain types of information and constraints. Thus, knowing how others have responded enables the individual to change his bid, thus testing for so-called "strategic bias" in responses. Approaches with such information may then be compared to approaches without that information. Nor has there been any "grand design" for questionnaires – they have varied because many different researchers have been involved and for differing purposes.

ii) Biases in CVM

A very large part of the literature on CVM is taken up with discussion about the "accuracy" of CVM. Accuracy is not easy to define. But since the basic aim of CVM is to elicit "real" values, a bid will be accurate if it coincides (within reason) with one that would result if an actual market existed. But since actual markets do not exist *ex hypothesi* (otherwise there would be no reason to use the technique), accuracy must be tested by seeing that

- The resulting bid is similar to that achieved by other techniques based on surrogate markets (house price approach, wage studies, etc.);
- The resulting bid is similar to one achieved by introducing the kinds of incentives that exist in real markets to reveal preference.

The issues are complex. For example, agreement between approaches may not mean much if there is no reason to suppose the surrogate market approaches are "accurate". A great deal of effort is thus expended in trying to ensure that incentives for "telling the truth" are present in the design of CVM techniques. The "accuracy" issue is discussed at length in Cummings, Brookshire and Schulze (1984).

There are various ways of classifying the nature of the biases that may be present in the CVM. Recent work tends to classify the biases as shown below in Table 10.

The concern with *strategic bias* is long standing in economics, and emanates from the supposed problem of getting individuals to reveal their true preferences in contexts where, by not telling the truth, they will still secure a benefit in excess of the costs they have to pay. This is the "free rider" problem (Samuelson 1954). For example, if individuals are told that a service will be provided if a) the total aggregated sum they are willing

Table 10. Source of bias in CVM

Strategic	Incentive to "free ride"?
Design	a) Starting Point Bias; b) Vehicle Bias; c) Informational Bias;
Hypothetical	Are bids in hypothetical markets different to actual market bids? Why should they be?
Operational	How are hypothetical markets consistent with markets in which actual choices are made?

to pay exceeds the cost of provision, and b) that each will be charged a price according to their maximum WTP, then the presumption is that each individual will understate his or her true demand. The context is one in which the good in question is a "public good", or has features of a public good. Such goods are difficult to provide in a way that excludes anyone from enjoying them, and the consumption of the good by each individual tends not to be at the cost of consumption to other individuals. Environmental quality has these features. Hence the relevance of the free rider problem.

The approach for testing strategic bias tends to be one in which the distribution of bids is regarded as following a "normal" distribution, or one consistent with the distribution of income. If the distribution of actual bids deviates significantly from these assumed distributions, strategic bias exists. In fact, both laboratory experiments and, perhaps less persuasively, CVM studies find little or no evidence of strategic bias [see, for example, Mitchell and Carson (1981)].

The potential for *design bias* arises from various sources. The first of these is *starting point bias*. It will be recalled that the interviewer suggests the first bid, the starting point. It is possible that this will influence the respondent in some way, perhaps by suggesting the range over which the "bidding game" would be played by the interviewer, perhaps by causing the respondent to agree too readily with bids in the vicinity of the initial bid in order to keep the game as short as possible.

CVM studies have attempted to test for this source of bias, usually by offering different starting bids, and sometimes by letting the respondent make the first bid. Statistically, then, it is possible to see if the mean (average) bid is affected by the choice of starting bid. The results are not conclusive: some studies [e.g. Thayer (1981)] finding no correlation between starting bids and mean bids, others, e.g. Boyle et al. (1985), finding that mean bids were very much affected by starting bids.

Vehicle bias arises from the choice of the "vehicle", or instrument of payment, used in the approach. Such vehicles include changes in local taxes, entrance fees, surcharges on bills (e.g. electricity bills), higher prices for goods, and so on. Respondents may be "sensitive" to the vehicle, perhaps regarding $1 paid through taxes as being more costly than $1 paid through an entrance fee.

The tests for vehicle bias are conceptually very simple. The average bid should not differ significantly between type of vehicle – e.g. the value of an improvement to the environment should be roughly the same whether the hypothetical payment is a tax increase or an entrance fee to the area, etc. If mean bids do vary by type of vehicle, vehicle bias may be said to exist. There are exceptions to this basic rule, but tests of the rule – by seeing how mean bids do vary with choice of instrument – seem to suggest some source of bias. The research issue that arises is then how to choose a "neutral" vehicle.

Information bias may arise from various aspects of the CVM. Starting point bias, for example, could be regarded as a form of information bias since it is the interviewer who "informs" the respondent of the first bid. The sequence in which information is supplied may also influence respondents – e.g. indicating the "importance" of a feature before explaining the nature of the choice. The general amount and quality of information is also of significance, particularly if the total cost of the environmental improvement is included in the information. The tests for such bias are difficult and usually involve either withholding information from one group and supplying it to another, or measuring the degree of information thought to be held by respondents. Various studies suggest no effect, while others [see the study by Schulz (1985a) discussed below] derive measured differences in WTP according to information differences.

Hypothetical bias. The basic idea of CVM is to elicit hypothetical bids that conform to actual bids if only actual markets exist. The basic difference between actual and hypothetical markets is that in actual markets purchasers will suffer a cost if they get it wrong – regret at having paid too much, for example. One obvious test is to carry out the CVM using hypothetical *and* actual payments. An example is provided by Bishop, Heberlein and Kealey (1983) in which Canada goose hunting was evaluated both in terms of the contingent responses of hunting permit holders and their actual cash offers. The comparison was between two measures of willingness to *accept* WTA, since goose hunters were offered bribes for their permits. The study found that hypothetical and actual valuations did differ significantly, with hypothetical WTA being less than actual WTA. This suggests that the hypothetical measures are "unreal", which is evidence of hypothetical bias. However, these results have been challenged in studies with the data reworked.

A study by Coursey *et al.* (1985) sought WTP and WTA to accept or forego repeated doses of an unpleasant (but harmless) liquid (sucrose octa acetate). The Coursey team found that as the doses were repeated, WTA and WTP tended to converge. The initial divergence between WTA and WTP was also found to be significantly greater when hypothetical values were sought than when actual payments were involved, again suggesting hypothetical bias. Other studies are less conclusive, but one survey of the CVM concludes that:

> "...one would tentatively conclude that compelling reasons exist for expecting biases in hypothetical valuations of the sort obtained in the CVM, relative to individual values that would obtain under conditions where expressed valuations must, in fact, be paid," [Cummings, Brookshire and Schulze (1984), p. 65].

Operational bias may be described in terms of the extent to which the actual "operating conditions" in the CVM approximate actual market conditions. This has led researchers to suggest various "Reference Operating Conditions" (ROCs) which should be met. The lists vary but all would include the requirement that respondents be familiar with the good they are being asked to value, and that they have either prior experience of varying the quantities of the good, or can "learn" how to do this through repeated bids. One might add to the list the requirement for the general absence of uncertainty, but it is worth noting that this automatically raises problems for the use of CVM in eliciting option values which arise precisely because of uncertainty.

iii) Comparisons of CVM Benefit Estimate Techniques with Other Techniques

It was noted above that the concept of "accuracy" is a little elusive when considering benefit measurement techniques. But some reassurance is likely to derive from any discovery that differing techniques secure similar valuations. Table 11 (next page) summarises several studies that have attempted such comparisons.

The seven studies shown compared CVM with one or other of the travel cost method (TCM) (see Chapter 4.5), hedonic property price approach (HPM = house price method), and site substitution approach (not discussed in this report). The *ranges* of values all overlap if accuracy is expressed as +– 60 per cent of the estimates shown, and overlap in 13 of the 15 comparisons if the range is +– 50 per cent. These are familiar ranges of error in estimates of demand functions in economics. This does not mean that the CVM is "correct" since, as noted above, we have in turn to make some judgment as to how correct the comparator techniques are. But it does tend to be reassuring.

iv) Uncovering Existence Values with the CVM

One significant feature of the CVM literature has been its use to elicit the different kinds of valuation that people place on environmental goods. In particular, CVM has suggested that existence values (see Chapter 3) may be very important. Schulze *et al.*

Table 11. **Comparisons of CVM with other techniques**

Study	CVM Results		Indirect market study	
	Commodity	Value[1]	Method	Value[1]
Knetsch & Davis (1966)	Recreation days	$1.71 per household/day	TCM	$ 1.66 per household/day
Bishop & Heberlein (1979)	Hunting permits	21 $ per permit	TCM	
			Value of time=0	$ 11.00
			Value of time=1/4 median inc.	$ 8.00
			Value of time=½ median inc.	$ 45.00
Desvouges, Smith and McGivney (1983)	Water quality improvements:	User values[2] Average (across question format)	TCM	User values
	a) Loss of use;	$21.41		$ 82.65
	b) Boatable to fishable;	$12.26		$ 7.01
	c) Boatable to swimmable	$29.64		$ 14.71
Seller, Stoll et Chavas (1984)	Boat permit to:	Close-ended consumer surplus	TCM	Consumer surplus:
	Lake Conroe	$39.38		$ 32.06
	Lake Livingstone	$35.21		$102.09
	Lake Houston	$13.01		$ 13.81
Thayer (1981)	Recreation site	Population value per household per day: $2.54	Site substitution	Population value per household per day: $2.04
Brookshire et al. (1982)	Air quality improvements:	Monthly value[3]	HPM (Property values)	Monthly value:
	a) Poor to fair;	$14.54		$ 45.92
	b) Fair to good.	$20.31		$ 59.09
Cummings et al. (1983)	Municipal infrastructure in:	Elasticity of substitution of wages for infrastructure	HPM (wages)	Elasticity of substitution of wages for infrastructure; 29 municipalities:
	a) Grants, New Mexico	−0.037		
	b) Farmington, New Mexico	−0.040		−0.035
	c) Sheridan, Wyoming	−0.042		
Brookshire et al. (1984)	Natural hazards (earthquakes) information	47 $ per month	HPM (Property values)	$37 par mois

1. Mean values amongst respondents.
2. Values apply to post-iteration bids for users of the recreation sites.
3. Value for sample population.
Source: Cummings, Brookshire and Schulze (1984), p. 125.

(1983), for example, have suggested that the benefits of preserving visibility in the Grand Canyon, United States are of the order of $3.5 billion per year, and some $6.2 billion per year if the visibility is extended to the southwestern parklands of the United States. Making allowance for future population trends, annualised benefits rise to $7.4 billion. These compare with the control costs of some $3 billion per year. This result comes from a CVM study in which photographs are used to depict the potential improvements and in which the vehicle for (hypothetical) payment was increases in electricity utility charges.

In a later paper, Brookshire et al. (1985) expand on the finding relating to the Grand Canyon. By looking at the bids made by respondents to experience improved visibility (regardless of whether visits take place or not), the authors find that the total "preservation bid" for the Grand Canyon's visibility was $4.43 per month, compared to a "user bid" of $0.07 per month. Interpreting existence value as the difference between total preservation value and use value, the finding is thus that existence value dominates preservation in this case. Existence value stands in the ratio of 66:1 to user values. (Note that what is being preserved is visibility, not the site itself.) The explanation for such a large ratio is that the resource in question is unique – it has no substitutes. Where substitutes exist one would expect existence values to be lower, and this tends to be the picture in other studies on existence value.

Strand (1981) reports a CVM-type study of acid rain for Norway. After indicating the nature of the environmental problem – damage to freshwater fish from acid rain – respondents were given a starting point figure for the global cost of stopping acid pollution which was translated into a special income tax. They were then asked if they were willing to pay this sum. The approach was thus of the "take-it-or-leave-it" kind rather than one involving iterative bids in which respondents could vary their bid according to different levels of clean-up. But the hypothetical tax rates were varied across the four samples of respondents interviewed – i.e. the tax rate was the same for each sample but varied between samples. The "yes" responses were found for the lower taxes. Strand then estimates "bid curves" using this information in a conditional probability framework – i.e. estimating the probability that a respondent would pay a particular tax given a certain income. Strand estimates that the average bid was 800 Norwegian Krone per capita. Given a population of 3.1 million, this translates to a "national" benefit of 2.5 billion Krone p.a. Earlier work by Strand suggests that user values are about 1 billion Krone, so that subtracting this from the implied total preservation value of 2.5 billion Krone gives an existence value of 1.5 billion Krone. In 1982 terms this translates to some $270 million p.a. or about 1 per cent of the Norwegian GNP. Note that, by asking for WTP, the Strand study probably underestimates the true value of benefits of reduced aquatic acidification. The reason for this is that a good deal of the acidity arises from "imported" pollution and respondents will generally have been aware of this. Accordingly, they may well have had the attitude that others besides themselves should pay for the clean-up.

v) Willingness to Pay VERSUS Willingness to Accept

The CVM has been particularly instrumental in a debate over the relationship between WTP and WTA measures of environmental change. It will be recalled that WTP is generally elicited when considering the valuation of a potential environmental *benefit*, whereas WTA seems more appropriate if we are asking someone to "accept" a *cost*. If we take a given state of the environment, then, we could ask for the WTP to improve the environment still further and the WTA to reduce environmental quality from the initial position. Eco-

nomic theory tells us that these two values should not differ significantly. Yet the CVM studies tend to suggest quite major disparities. Table 12 shows some examples of the kinds of differences that have been found.

How are the differences to be explained? There are various options. The main ones are:

i) Economic theory is wrong and people value gains and losses "asymmetrically", attaching a lot more weight to a loss compared to the existing position than to a gain;

ii) The relevant CVM studies are flawed and no reliance can be placed in the disparate estimates;

iii) CVM studies tend to deal with large, discrete changes and "instant" valuations. These cannot be compared to the context in which economic theory concludes that WTA and WTP must be very similar.

The literature is divided on which explanation is correct; proposition *i)*, in particular, exciting considerable controversy. Psychologists such as Kahneman and Tversky (1979) suggest that *prospect theory* explains a good deal of the difference. In prospect theory individuals' values relate to gains and losses in comparison to some "reference point". This contrasts with the economic assumption that individuals maximise "utility". What matters is the point from which the gains and losses are measured. This may, for example, be the

Table 12. **Disparities between WTP and WTP**[a]

Study		WTP	WTA
Hammack and Brown (1974)	(1)	247.00	1 044.00
Banford, Knetsch & Mauser (1977)	(2)	43.00	120.00
		22.00	93.00
Sinclair (1976)		35.00	100.00
Bishop & Heberlein (1979)[b]		21.00	101.00
Brookshire, Randall & Stoll (1980)	(1)	43.64	68.52
	(2)	54.07	142.60
	(3)	32.00	207.07
Rowe, d'Arge & Brookshire (1980)	(1)	4.75	24.47
	(2)	6.54	71.44
	(3)	3.53	46.63
	(4)	6.85	113.68
Coursey, Shulze & Hovis (1983)	(1)	2.50	9.50
	(2)	2.75	4.50
Knetsch & Sinden (1983)	(1)	1.28	5.18

a) All figures are in year-of-study dollars. The bracketed numbers refer to either the number of valuations received or the number of trials (in experiments) conducted.
b) Mitchell and Carson (1984) re-estimated Bishop and Heberlein's results with contrary conclusions.
Source: Cummings, Brookshire and Schulze (1984), p. 42.

status quo. Second, prospect theory suggests that values for negative deviations from the reference point will be greater than values placed on positive deviations. Gains will be valued less than losses, just as the CVM studies suggest. Third, the manner in which the gains and losses are to be secured matters a great deal. An "imposed" loss for example will tend to attract a much higher value than a voluntarily secured gain of equal quantity.

Similar points about the perception of gain and loss have been made by others [Thaler (1980)]; Gregory (1986). Thus, it is suggested that a loss of something that is already owned is regarded as more important than the gain of something not yet possessed; the regret attached to going without something one never had is less than the cost of losing what one already has.

A great deal more research is needed to investigate these issues. The issue is important, for if WTA and WTP really do differ by multiples of 3 or more (as the empirical literature suggests) then the kinds of values placed on the environment are similarly affected.

vi) A Case Study Using the CVM

An interesting contingent valuation study has been carried out by Schulz (1985a) to measure the benefits of improved air quality in West Berlin. Berlin is subject to significant "smogs" and Germans in general have a heightened sensitivity to air pollution problems because of the extensive publicity given to forest damage from acid rain. Between 1980 and 1985 the first stage of the West Berlin smog alarm system was activated ten times, and early in 1985 the sulphur dioxide level caused a stage three alert in the Ruhr. Schulz issued a postal willingness-to-pay survey to some 4,500 Berliners in 1983, requesting responses about their perception of air quality, the extent to which they were knowledgeable about the effects of air pollution and the nature of air pollution, the extent to which air pollution had personally affected the respondent (in terms of health, property damage, etc.) together with the usual questions about willingness to pay. In turn, the WTP questions used two hypothetical payment "vehicles" : one in which polluters bore all the cost and the other in which the respondent could expect to pay for abatement measures. The air quality gradations were based on generalised measures ranging from "smog" through to "holiday air" (clean air), thus permitting respondents to identify fairly readily with the classifications. WTP questions were "closed" – i.e. open-ended responses were not generally permitted, but tests were carried out to see how much difference closed and open questions would make.

The results indicated some interesting features of WTP. First, the quantitative levels of WTP were very high. Extrapolated from the sample to Berlin in general and to the whole of Germany (using factor analysis which in turn suggested extrapolation on the basis of age – see below) the results indicate a West Berlin evaluation of clean air of DM 4.6 billion (about US $1.6 billion) and a German valuation of DM 138 billion (about

US $48 billion). In terms of percentages of GDP these are 7 per cent and 11 per cent respectively, remarkably high figures. In each case, the valuations relate to changes from severe air pollution (Berlin) or "city quality" (Germany) to clean air ("holiday air"). The second significant aspect of the results is the factors explaining the valuations. Age turned out to be very important; younger people placing significantly more value on clean air than older people. Knowledge about air pollution was also important; the greater the familiarity with the pollution process and the kinds of damage in which it is implicated the greater the valuations. The level of personal experience of damage also mattered; those with direct experience of corrosion, soiling or health damage giving higher valuations. Figure 5 shows the relationship between monetary values (in DM per month of WTP) and level of air quality. Note that Berliners have lower valuations than Germany due to the older age structure of Berlin compared to the nation as a whole. The higher valuations of the "informed" against "less informed" are also clear.

4.5. TRAVEL COST APPROACHES

i) Introduction

In Sections 4.2 and 4.3 we considered two direct methods of obtaining information on the individual's willingness to pay for environmental quality. The hedonic price and wage models discussed are market-related methods because they obtain the required information by reference to a market activity in which the individual is involved – the choice of residential location or occupation or both. In contrast the contingent valuation methods discussed in Section 4.4 approach the question by directly eliciting the information from the person concerned and do not involve any observable behaviour on the part of the individual or household. In this section we will examine another market-related method which is widely used to estimate the benefits of environmental improvements in recreational facilities such as parks, lakes, etc. The underlying idea of this method is to use information on the amount of money *and* time that people have spent in getting to a recreational site to estimate their willingness to pay for the facilities of that site. A number of models have been estimated within this general framework and these are collectively known as travel cost models (TCMs for short).

We will begin by describing the theory that lies behind these approaches and explaining what its limitations are. When the theory comes to be applied, there are inevitably corners that have to be cut. We next describe what these have been and what the likely impact of cutting them has been on the results obtained. In doing this we concentrate on one particular study undertaken

Figure 5

Willingness to Pay Schedule for Clean Air: Germany

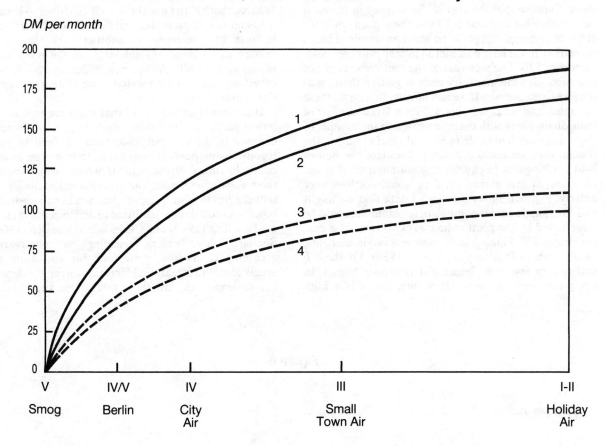

DM per month

1 = FRG (Informed)
2 = Berlin (Informed)
3 = FRG (Less Informed)
4 = Berlin (Less Informed)

in the United States by the Environmental Protection Agency as part of an exercise comparing TCMs and alternative methods of estimating benefits for water based recreational activities. This study [Desvousges, Smith and McGivney (1983) – henceforth the EPA (1983) report] addresses itself to a large number of the issues involved in the use of TCMs and is a useful indicator of the state of the art at the time it was undertaken. Finally we look at more recent developments in this area and try to evaluate the overall usefulness of this technique as a method of benefit estimation. Annex 6 describes the underlying model more fully and indicates which econometric techniques are appropriate for the estimation of the models.

ii) TCM – The Theory

Travel cost models are based on an extension of the theory of consumer demand in which special attention is paid to the value of time. That time is valuable is self evident. What precisely its value is, remains a question on which there is some disagreement, as will become clear later. However, as a starting point let us imagine a household consisting of a single person who works as a driver. He can work as many or as few hours as he wishes and he earns $5 an hour. He is fortunate enough not to pay taxes, and enjoys (or dislikes) driving for work or for recreation equally much. On a particular day he can either drive to a park that takes an hour to get to, and spend some time there, or he can go to work. In these circumstances he is faced with possibly two decisions. The first is whether to go to the park or to go to work. The second is, if he goes to the park, how much time to spend there. Suppose that the cost of the journey in terms of petrol and wear and tear is $3 and there is an entry fee of $1. If he goes to the park and spends a couple of hours there, then it will have cost him $4 in cash *plus* the loss of income of $20. The true cost of the visit consists of the entry fee, plus the monetary costs of getting there, plus the foregone earnings. If we had information on all these variables, and we could obtain it for a large number of individuals, along with the information on the number of visits that each had made (and would make) during the season, then we could attempt to estimate the household's willingness to pay for a given number of visits. However, at first glance the data would not look very orderly. Figure 6 shows the kind of data that we might find. Our single earner household, for example, could be represented by the point *a*: he makes 10 visits at a cost per visit of $20. Points *b* and *c* represent two households, each of whom face very high costs ($30). Of these *b* makes very few visits because it is a poor household living far from the recreational site, and *c* is a high

earning household located near the park that makes a lot of short visits (being a high earner it has a high foregone earnings component to its costs). Points *d*, *e* and *f* also represent households with the same costs per visit. Whereas both *d* and *e* make few visits, *d* does so because it has no attraction to the facilities offered, but *e* does so because he has access to another park close to its residential location. Household *f*, on the other hand, makes a lot of visits. Although it is identical to *e* in every other respect, it is not located close to another recreational area.

It is clear from the above that if we are to trace out how a particular household, such as *a*, would react to changes in the cost per visit, then we need to group together households that are similar to *a*. The locus of points linking such households would then constitute their *demand curve* for the recreational facilities that that site has to offer. [The seminal works demonstrating how travel cost data can be used to derive demand curves are Hotelling (1949) and Clawson and Knetsch (1966).] Similarity here means grouping our observations according to income, preference for recreation and access to other recreational facilities. Given the demand curves we can calculate the benefits of the site by taking

Figure 6

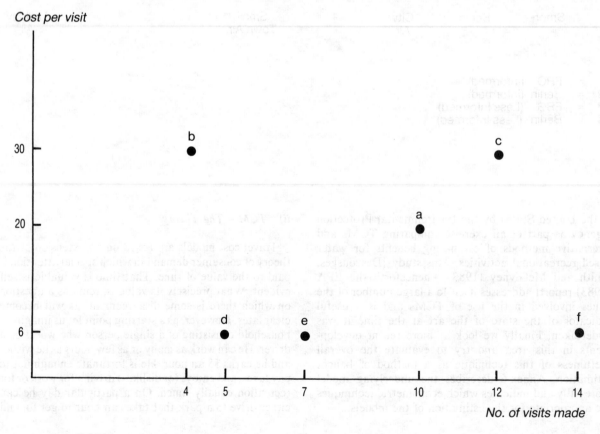

the area under these curves to obtain the consumer surplus as indicated in Chapter Two. Adding up the consumer surpluses for different categories of households gives us the overall benefit of the site.

If the model developed here is to be used to evaluate the benefits of environmental *improvements*, then further work has to be done. It is no longer enough to separate out the groups according to what other recreational facilities they may have access to. We now need to know how much of the willingness to pay of a category of households will increase if the facility at a particular site is improved to allow, for example, the possibility of fishing in a lake where none was possible before. This in turn requires knowledge of how much of the willingness to pay for each site is due to each of its specific facilities. Then by looking across sites we will be able to trace out changes in this willingness to pay as facilities change. The data required for such an exercise would include the facilities of each site and the location of each household relative to all the sites. This is clearly a very large amount of information and so some simplifying assumptions will be necessary in many cases. What these are

and how they affect the results is discussed later in this section.

If we can derive the demand curve for recreation for a particular category of households defined by household characteristics such as income, education and the liking for recreational facilities, and we can show how this demand curve would shift if facilities improved, then the benefit of the improvement can be derived as shown in Figure 7. AB is the curve prior to the change and CD is the curve after the change. The benefits of this group of consumers are given by the area ABCD. Adding across groups gives the total benefit.

iii) TCM – Methods of Estimation

In this section we discuss some of the specific problems of estimating the demand for recreational services. Before doing that, however, we should note that although the model outlined above assumes a variable number of visits per household, a somewhat different

Figure 7

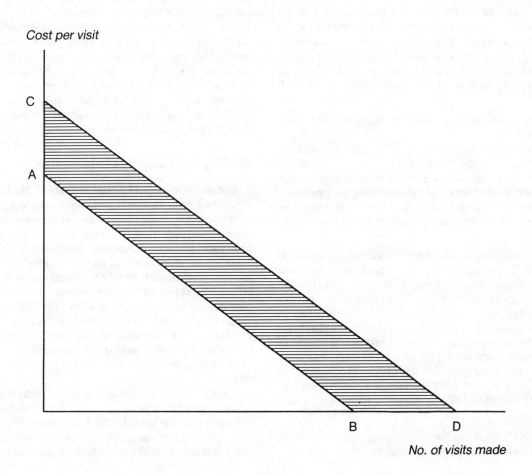

demand curve can also be estimated with, say, only one visit per household to the site. This would be done by looking at the differences in visitation rates for households in different zones and calculating the probability of a visit for a household with given income and other characteristics, living a certain distance from the site. The basic problems of estimation are similar for the two models and for expositional reasons we will continue to look at the multi-visit model. These problems can be examined under the following headings:

a) Data on travel costs and travel times;
b) Data on household characteristics;
c) Data on recreational facilities;
d) Specification of the demand relationship;
e) Estimation problems.

a) Data on Travel Costs and Travel Times

The cost of visiting a site consists of the transportation costs plus the opportunity costs of the time taken for the journey and the time spent at the site. The earliest studies of the demand for recreation ignored the opportunity costs of time [Clawson and Knetsch (1966)]. Doing this is going to result in biased estimates as was realised early on in the work on TCMs. Those making fewer visits because of high time costs will be deemed to have a low willingness to pay for the number of visits that they do make and so the estimated demand curve in Figure 7 will be flatter than the true demand curve. Hence some estimate of the time taken for the journey to the park is essential. The next question is, what value should we place on each hour of travel time? In our earlier example we suggested that it might be the wage of the person making the journey. However, in reality:

i)   One is not free to work during the time spent on the journey;
ii) The wage rate paid and the amount received are not equal due to taxation;
iii) There is a psychic cost to work which is not the same as that incurred when driving to a park;
iv) The loss of earnings may be more than one person's, if the family consists of multiple earners.

These issues were all assumed away in our artificial example. In a review of many studies of travel time and transportation cost, Cesario (1976) concluded that the value of travel time was somewhere between one quarter and one half of the wage rate. This would mean that in estimating the number of visits as a function of the travel cost and other variables, the travel cost would consist of the transportation costs, plus (approximately) one third of the hourly wage times the hours taken to complete the journey. In the EPA (1983) study this assumption was tested by estimating the demand for travel with travel costs:

i) Calculated using the actual wage;
ii) Calculated using one third of the wage; and

iii) With the proportion of the wage left to be determined by the estimation procedure.

On the whole it was found that there was greater support for using the actual wage than one third of the wage, but there were cases where it would have been better to allow the coefficient to be freely determined by the estimation procedure.

The other time variable which is of importance is the time spent at the site. As we stated at the beginning, the decisions of how many visits to make and how long each visit should be are taken jointly. In some cases the problems of visits of different length have been tackled by separating the data into, for example, weekday and weekend visits (Cicchetti, Fisher & Smith (1976). Otherwise the assumption of a constant time spent by each visitor on each visit is generally made. This can result in biases if the time spent varies systematically with the distance travelled. For example, if those who come from further away spend less time at the site, then their time costs will be lower per visit relative to those who come from nearby. This will mean that ignoring these costs will make the demand curve in Figure 7 steeper than it really is. The converse will be true if the time spent increases with distance.

The EPA study cited above tried to check for the bias that ignoring onsite time might cause. It estimated the demand for visits both when onsite time was included and when it was excluded. Twenty-three sites were looked at, and in five of these the inclusion of onsite time had a small but statistically significant *negative* impact on the estimated number of visits made. More importantly, however, the estimated slope of the demand curve in Figure 7 was generally unaffected by the inclusion of onsite time costs. Taken together, these findings suggest that ignoring onsite time costs is unlikely to result in serious errors of estimation of the demand for recreational benefits.

b) Data on Household Characteristics

The main household variable that TCMs include in their analysis is income. Economic theory suggests that as income increases, so does the willingness to pay for recreational facilities. However, most studies find that although the income variable generally has the right "sign" (i.e. willingness to pay is positively related to income) the magnitude of the coefficient is small and frequently statistically insignificant. This result was particularly noticeable in the EPA (1983) study. Other variables that have been included on the household side are the age of the head of household, a measure of education and some measure of the subjective strength of preference for the particular kind of recreation being offered.

Another use to which data on household characteristics has been put is to obtain an estimate of the *wage* of the head of household. In the EPA study, for example, data on income was gathered from recreational site users, but this is not the same as the hourly wage. Indeed it is very rare for data on the latter to be directly available. What the EPA study did was to use an independently estimated hedonic wage equation to obtain estimates of the influence of education, race, sex, age, location, etc., on the hourly wage and then use the respondents' data on these variables to predict their hourly wage. This predicted value was then used in the calculation of the travel costs. This procedure is employed in many contexts and, as long as the underlying hedonic wage equation is properly estimated, it should yield satisfactory results.

c) Data on Recreational Facilities

Data on the "facilities" available include variables such as land area, shore miles, pool elevation and the number of multipurpose recreation areas on the site. All of these were considered in the EPA study. In addition data on water quality were also gathered. These included variables such as temperature, pH, dissolved oxygen and turbidity. The effects of these facilities on the demand for the services of a site is measured [following Freeman (1979b)] in two stages. The first estimates the number of visits to site i as a function of household characteristics only. For example the following equation is estimated:

$$V_i = \alpha_0 + \alpha_1 TC_i + \alpha_2 INC_i$$

where,

V_i is the number of visits to the site by respondent i,

TC_i is the total travel cost of respondent i to the site,

INC_i is the income of respondent i.

α_0, α_1, α_2, are the coefficients to be estimated. These equations are run and the values of α obtained for each site j. The second stage is to explain the variation in each of the as across the sites by using the site characteristics. The EPA study estimated the α for 46 sites using a semi log form of the above equation and then estimated a set of equations in which each of the as was regressed on the size of the site, its number of access points, its water quality, etc.. It was found that if those sites with particular statistical problems were excluded, then variation in α_1 (the travel cost coefficient) could be explained well by some of the site characteristics, but that neither the intercept term α_0 nor the income term α_2 could be so explained. Given that α_2 was poorly determined anyway, lack of success in explaining its variation is not surprising. α_1 was most influenced by the number of shore miles on the site, the number of recreation areas, the ratio of water to land area, and the mean and variance of the dissolved oxygen levels in the water. The last two were the only significant environmental variables found in the study, and they had the sign that one would expect – i.e. an improvement in water quality would shift the demand curve outwards.

d) Specification of the Demand Relationship

After trying a number of specifications, it was found that the equation for V_i was best estimated in a semi log form – i.e. with V_i replaced by its logarithm in that equation. The second set of equations discussed above were estimated as linear equations. One of the problems of environmental benefit estimation is that while the final numbers can be quite sensitive to the precise form of the demand relationship that is assumed, the statistical techniques cannot discriminate between the different specifications. It is encouraging therefore to come across a clear preference for one specification of the demand equation.

e) Estimation Problems

The statistical issues involved in the estimation of TCMs are complex and cannot be discussed in much detail without a prior understanding of econometric models. As far as a survey of this nature is concerned, however, a number of points should be noted. The first of these has already been discussed. This is the matter of the joint determination of the number of visits and length of visits. We have seen that, in principle, ignoring the latter in the determination of the former could lead to biases. However, in a careful examination of the data the EPA (1983) study found that the effects of the omission on the estimated demand curve were either small or insignificant or both. Whether this result will hold in other studies remains to be seen.

The second point of importance is the treatment of the number of visits. In reality this variable can only take discrete non-negative values, such as 0,1,2.... The technique of estimation, however, assumes that it is a continuous variable that can take negative or positive values. The appropriate procedure with discrete multivalued data such as we have here is the use of discrete estimating procedures such as the multinomial logit or the poisson distribution. Some work using these is now being done but it is not yet possible to evaluate its implications for the results obtained in TCMs.

Finally, an issue that is of general importance needs to be considered. In any data set where we have information on a number of respondents who have actually *visited* a site, we are of course lacking corresponding information on others who have not visited the site. At first glance this might seem immaterial to the estimation of the demand for the site, but a more careful consideration will show that a bias is likely to result.

Figure 8 shows us the pattern of visits for a particular category of households. The estimated line (E) is drawn to give a best fit to the pattern of observations. However at high travel costs there will be a cluster of people who will have made no visits. Had they been included, the effect would have been to shift the line to (T) as shown in Figure 8, because of the weight of the cluster in pulling the line up on the vertical axis. This particular source of bias, known as truncation bias, has been investigated in many econometric applications and found to be quite

Figure 8

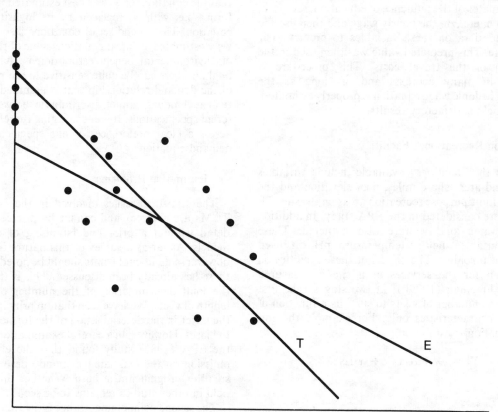

Cost per visit

No. of visits made

serious. In the EPA (1983) study the authors tried to evaluate it using an approximate correction factor, and found that, of the 46 sites looked at, about 11 had serious truncation biases. Furthermore when these sites were eliminated from the data set, the results of the second stage of the analysis were both more plausible and better determined.

The importance of dealing properly with the truncation bias has been further stressed by Smith and Desvousges (1985). Developing their work in the EPA study, the authors looked at the bias caused *both* by excluding those with zero visits as well as setting those with more than 6 visits at 6 visits. Using an estimation technique which explicitly took account of these factors they reestimated the original model. They found that the parameters obtained were significantly different; with the revised figures suggesting a much more elastic demand for recreational visits and thereby a much smaller consumer surplus associated with site values. The second stage equations also showed substantially different results. Although dissolved oxygen was still found to be the best water quality variable, it now affected only the intercept term significantly. Further-

more, the factors which had previously been found to have a significant effect on the α's (the number of shore miles, the number of access points, etc.) were now found generally not to be significant. This reevaluation of their own work would seem to suggest that the issue of the appropriate specification and choice of variables is not settled. However, one important finding was that if one recalculated the environmental benefits of an improvement in the dissolved oxygen levels, the results of the two sets of estimates were considerably closer than the estimates themselves would suggest. The differences in the numerical values of the estimates of the two stages appear to have offsetting effects, leaving the welfare implications of the earlier study much more intact.

iv)   Conclusions

Travel cost models are an important direct method of evaluating the demand for recreational facilities, and for valuing the changes in such facilities brought about by environmental improvements. Since the earliest work in this area by Clawson (1959), the techniques used have steadily improved and a number of theoretical and empirical issues have been tackled. The results obtained by the use of these models are encouraging and broadly similar to those obtained by other methods. For example, some comfort can be drawn from the fact that when the results of TCMs are compared with those of contingent valuation methods, then the 'differences are not substantial and fall within the range of variation of the contingent valuation methods across the question formats" [EPA (1983) pp. 8-21]. On theoretical grounds one would expect that consumer surplus measures such as those derived from TCM demand curves would provide an upper limit to the willingness to pay as calculated by the CV method. At present our estimation techniques and our data are not accurate enough to be able to test this proposition. Nevertheless, it is interesting to note, as Bishop and Heberlein (1979) have done, that, with plausible values of the opportunity cost of travel time, the results of the two methods are quite close.

However, in spite of these positive results, there are still a number of reservations about the applicability of this technique. It requires a very large amount of data which are expensive to collect and codify. Also it assumes that any travel undertaken to a site is solely for the purpose of visiting that site. If the trips are multi-purpose ones, then the division of the costs between the purposes becomes arbitrary and the method is no longer suitable. Finally, on the technical side, changes in estimating methods are still going on and their implications for the estimates are still unclear. Hence the methodology has not yet reached a stage where a standard application "package" can be used with confidence.

In conclusion we would say that TCMs are a useful tool for valuing recreational benefits in situations where sites are visited by a broad range of users specifically for recreational purposes and where adequate data on the characteristics of the site and the user are available.

Chapter 5

INDIRECT VALUATION PROCEDURES

5.1. INTRODUCTION

Indirect procedures for benefit estimation do not seek to measure direct revealed preferences for the environmental good in question. Instead, they calculate a "dose-response" relationship between pollution and some effect, and only then is some measure of preference for that effect applied. Examples of dose-response relationships include the effect of pollution on health; the effect of pollution on the physical depreciation of material assets such as metals and buildings; the effect of pollution on aquatic ecosystems, and the effect of pollution on vegetation. Note that some of these environmental damages can be valued directly. Thus we have seen an example in which the contingent valuation method is used to value the effects of acid pollution on rivers and lakes in Norway (Chapter 4.4).

The dose-response approach tends to be used when it is thought that people are unaware of the effects that pollution causes. In general, dose-response approaches are always applicable to environmental problems. That is, if there is some damage and it is linked to a cause, the relationship between that cause and effect is dose-response linkage. This does not mean it can be estimated with any precision: it simply states that a physical relationship exists. Direct approaches, however, will not result in "true" damage or benefit estimates if people are unaware of the linkages. A checklist is provided below.

A "Y" indicates that the approach is applicable in principle, an "O" that it is not, and "T" indicates that awareness is likely to occur only after a significant threshold has been reached. It will be evident that direct procedures can be applied only in certain cases. Material damage, for example, could be valued directly since people are generally aware of the extent of corrosion done to buildings. On the other hand they are less likely to be aware of the damage being done to structures generally, or to metals. In the global context, while we could seek people's reaction to CFC (chlorofluorocarbon) damage, the amount of information required is rather substantial and it is far more likely that will we use an indirect approach.

Once the dose-response relationship is established, indirect approaches then utilise valuations which are applied to the "responses". In the health example, it would be a value of life that is applied to market values of depreciation in the materials, plus some adjustment for surplus, and so on. Dose-response approaches estimate *damage* actually done. They show, for example, the number of fatalities due to sulphur oxide pollution, the rate of building depreciation due to acid pollution, and so on.

A "damage function" relates physical damage done to the level of pollution, and a "monetary damage function" is then the physical damage function multiplied by a unit "price" (value) per unit of physical damage. (We abstract from situations in which the relationships are not linear.) To find a measure of the monetary benefit of an environmental policy, then, it is necessary to proceed as follows:

i) Estimate a physical damage function of the form

$$R = R(P, \text{other variables})$$

where R is the physical damage (the response), P is pollution;

ii) Calculate the coefficient of R on P through multiple regression analysis (typically) – i.e. calculate $\Delta R / \Delta P$ (where Δ means "change in");

iii) Calculate the change in pollution due to the environmental policy – i.e. calculate ΔP;

Table 13. **Dose-response linkage and benefit estimation**

Type of Linkage	Awareness ?	
	Yes (Use direct procedures)	No (Use indirect procedures)
Air pollution – Health	O	Y
Accidents – Health	Y	Y
Water Pollution – Health	O	Y
Air Pollution – Materials	?	Y
Air Pollution – Crops	T	Y
Air Pollution – Soiling	Y	Y
Air Pollution – Trees	T	Y
Global Pollution:		
CFC Damage	O	Y
CO_2 Damage	O	Y

iv) Calculate V. Δ P. Δ R/Δ P = V.Δ R = Δ D, where Δ D is the "damage avoided" by the environmental policy and is thus equal to the benefits of the policy.

A "broad brush" approach to indirect valuation can be illustrated, using Dutch estimates of damage done by acid rain. Damage done to soils from acidification requires offsetting by the use of lime dressings. These additional dressings are estimated to cost between Gld. 15-50 million. Systematic crop reductions account for a further Gld. 30-300 million, while "acute" episodes might add a further Gld. 0.3-30 million. Annual costs of maintaining heather fields in nature reserves are put at Gld. 3-30 million. Allowing for the future loss of stock of nature areas, the costs of reestablishing could be Gld. 10-25 million in future years. Forest losses are not directly estimated in terms of the damage currently occurring, but the losses would include both timber yield reductions and recreational and ecological values. Loss of forest stock, however, could run to Gld. 3-10 billion, which, when annutised into a cost of reestablishing the lost stock, could cost Gld. 150-500 million.

"Cultural" goods such as historic buildings are also damaged by acidification. Restoration and protection costs Gld. 25-40 million p.a. An estimated backlog of past damage (in terms of restoration costs) is annutised to a cost of Gld. 30-60 million. Groundwater effects of acidification are speculative, but a broad indicator is that one-third of groundwater for drinking and industrial supplies will be affected in the near future.

Table 14. **Some estimates of acidification damage in the Netherlands**

1983/84 Gld. millions

	Current damage	Future damage
Agriculture:		
Extra liming	15-50	15-50
Crop yield	30-300	30-300
Acute crop damage	0.3-3	0.3-3
Land ecosystems:		
Extra management	3-30	3-30
Forestry:		
Management	n.a.	n.a.
Timber yields	n.a.	20-50
Stock loss	n.a.	150-500
Recreation	n.a.	n.a.
Cultural goods:		
Restoration	25-50	25-50
Past damage	30-60	30-60
Other goods	40	40
Drinking water	n.a.	20-50
Total	150-500	350- 1 100
Total (US$) (Using 1985 exchange rates)	44-145	102-319

Source: Ministry of Housing and Environment, Netherlands (1986).

Corrective policy would cost Gld. 20-50 million. Table 14 summarises the Dutch estimates. They are very rough but can be regarded as offering an "order of magnitude" estimate of damage.

5.2. POLLUTION AND HEALTH

i) Introduction

The procedure outlined above has been extensively used in health studies. The critical research effort is in the estimation of the dose-response relationship between ill-health and pollution. The usual procedure is to take a large database relating to ill-health, including mortality, and relate it to various factors which can be regarded as being likely to affect the indicator of ill-health. Such approaches are sometimes referred to as "macroepidemiology" because they use data sets that are significantly larger than those that an epidemiologist, seeking to control as many factors as possible, would use.

A regression equation is formed which links health damage or mortality to factors such as income, race, diet, education, age, smoking habits, pollution levels, and so on. The coefficient linking the health indicator to pollution is then the equivalent of R/P in the preceding discussion. In the early studies, the equations were simplistic, partly because of the novelty of the research and partly because of the data limitations. Improved data sets and considerable research effort have meant that recent studies are very much more sophisticated.

The pioneering work in macroepidemiology is that of Lave and Seskin (1973, 1977), the results of which have been brought up to date in Chappie and Lave (1983). This work has occasioned substantial comment and critical appraisal centering on issues relating to the air pollution data used, omitted variables, the form in which the multiple regression equation is specified, the econometric problems involved, and so on [see Gerking and Schulze (1981), Crocker *et al.* (1979), Lipfert (1979) and Thibodeau *et al.* (1980), among many others].

ii) Air Pollution and Mortality

Virtually all the macroepidemiological work relating air pollution to mortality and morbidity has been carried out in the United States. One of the data sets used by Lave and Seskin (1977) has been reevaluated by Lipfert (1984). The data are for 1969 for Standard Metropolitan Statistical Areas (SMSAs).Lipfert modified the Lave and Seskin analysis to include improved data, new variables [some of which are, however, included in the Chappie and Lave (1983) extension of the earlier Lave and Seskin work], different specifications of the mortality-pollution relationship, and additional statistical techniques.

Lave and Seskin found a statistically significant relationship between two air pollutants – sulphate (SO4) and particulates (total suspended particulates = TSP) – and mortality. As with most of the macroepidemiological studies, many regression equations are estimated. Just one is reported here simply to illustrate the nature of such an equation and the procedure for estimating monetary benefit. Lave and Seskin's equation relating unadjusted 1969 mortality data to a set of influencing variables was:

M = 3.31 + 0.657 (% < 65) + 0.0204 (% non-white) + 0.0557 (% poor) + 0.131 (pop den) − 0.365 (log pop) + 0.0082 TSP + 0.077 (min sulf).

In the equation:

M = mortality in terms of deaths per 1 000 people per (μ g/m^3) (a revision of the units used in the original Lave and Seskin work).

% < 65 = ·percentage of population under 65

pop den = a measure of population density

log pop = logarithm of population

min sulf = minimum values of sulphur pollution.

As it stands, the equation is not very revealing. However, it is possible to interpret the coefficients of TSP and min sulf in terms of elasticities, i.e. the percentage reduction in mortality that can be expected from a given percentage reduction in air pollution. Such elasticities have immediate policy relevance since pollution policy is often expressed in terms of target percentage reductions in emissions or concentrations.

In the above case, the calculation of the elasticity requires that the average (mean) level of mortality and the average levels of TSP and sulphur be known. These are reported in the Lave and Seskin study. Expressed in the same units as above, the relevant data are [Lave and Seskin (1977, p. 323)]:

Mean of mortality = M = 9.022 deaths
    per 1 000 population

Mean of minimum sulphur = S = 3.462 μ g/m^3

Mean of TSP = P = 95.58 μ g/m^3

The measurement for both pollutants combined is then

$$E = \frac{\Delta M.S}{\Delta S.M} + \frac{\Delta M.P}{\Delta P.M}$$

Substituting the values given, we have:

E = (1/9.022) [(0.077)(3.462) + (0.0082)(95.58)]
  = 0.116

This would suggest on Lave and Seskin's analysis that a 1 per cent reduction in air pollution will give rise to a 0.12 per cent reduction in mortality.

Lave and Seskin's original benefit estimate related to changes in air pollution between 1973 and 1979 in the United States. An 88 per cent reduction in sulphur oxide pollution and a 58 per cent reduction in particulate pollution should, using the separate elasticities for SO4 and TSP, produce a 7 per cent reduction in mortality. Applying some "value of life" estimates taken (and modified) from earlier work by Cooper and Rice (1976), Lave and Seskin conclude that this reduction in mortality translates to a monetary benefit of reduced pollution of $16.1 billion in 1973 price terms.

Lave and Seskin's work proved to be influential in terms of further research but also in terms of its impact on policy thinking. For example, it formed the basis for later work by the Council on Environmental Quality [Freeman (1982)]. It is important, then, to establish how far the work has stood the test of time.

Lipfert (1984) has improved the database and subjected the analysis to various alternative specifications of the regression equation. He reports the coefficients for various specifications and shows the sulphur coefficient is dramatically reduced when new variables are added. The coefficient even becomes statistically insignificant in a number of cases. Analysis with the additional variables and other corrections also suggests that smoking, drinking water quality and ozone pollution are significant.

On sulphate Lipfert concludes that:

"... the overall conclusion should be that sulphate regression coefficients are not to be taken seriously". [Lipfert (1984, p. 237).]

This is in marked contrast with Lave and Seskin's conclusion which implicates sulphur in mortality.

What happens to TSP? In general the size of the coefficient also falls as new variables are added and modified regression techniques are used, but it remains statistically significant. Nonetheless, Lipfert concludes that:

"Since sulfate and TSP interact with another (sic) in these regressions, caution is in order for TSP as well." (Ibid).

iii) Air Pollution and Morbidity

Lave and Seskin's work relate to the pollution-mortality relationship. They assume that the same relationship would hold for morbidity-illness. Subsequent to the Lave and Seskin work various studies have attempted separately to determine the pollution-morbidity link [Crocker et al. (1979)], Graves and Krumm (1981), Seskin (1979) and Portney and Mullahy (1983). A major study is that of Ostro (1983, 1987) to which we now turn.

Ostro uses data from the 1976 Health Interview Survey of the (United States) National Center for Health Statistics, a database covering 50 000 households. The health data is then matched to pollution data and other information from other sources, covering 84 SMSAs. Morbidity was measured in two ways –

i) By days absent from work, or "work loss days" (WLD);

ii) By indicators of days affected by ill-health, or "restricted activity days" (RAD).

The WLD measures relate to workers only, while RADs relates to workers and non-workers.

Ostro's procedure is then very much like that described above for the dose-response mortality studies. RAD and WLD are separately regressed on various variables, and for differing subgroups. Thus Ostro estimates equations for all people aged 18-65 in the sample, all workers, all non-smokers (to isolate any effects of smoking) and all male non-smokers. Taking the total sample we report below just the coefficients for particulates (TSP) and mean sulphur levels (SULF). The other variables included were number of chronic conditions, race, marriage, temperature, rainfall, population density, income, social status, sex, cigarette consumption and work status. It will be noted that no other air pollution variable was included (recall Lipfert's findings on ozone), nor any diet or water quality variable. The results for the total sample were:

$$RAD = -0.83 + 0.00282 \ TSP - 0.00008 \ SULF + ...$$

$$WLD = -0.47 + 0.00145 \ TSP - 0.001 \ SULF + ...$$

The sulphur coefficients are both non-significant and the wrong sign. Thus, Ostro's work is consistent with the mortality findings of Lipfert – sulphur is not implicated in ill-health or mortality (but bear in mind that sulfur and TSP are interlinked in that the former is part of the latter).

As with Lave and Seskin's work, it is possible to translate the TSP coefficients into elasticities. These are reported as 0.45 for WLD and 0.39 for RAD. Recall that this means a 1 per cent reduction in air pollution leads to a 0.45 per cent reduction in working days lost, and so on. The major significance of this finding is that such elasticities are some ten times the comparable elasticities that tended to emerge as the "consensus" mortality elasticities from the Lave and Seskin work [thus Freeman (1982) uses an elasticity of 0.04 based on his judgment of the Lave and Seskin work].

Ostro's initial study was replicated using Health Interview Survey data for 1976-1981. The replicated study also made several adjustments to the measures of health effects, and introduced a new measure of pollution based on fine particles (FP) as opposed to the more traditional TSP. In 4 of the 6 years (1976-1981) FP was found to be associated with working days lost (WLD), while the association between FP and RAD was significant in all 6 years.

Ostro does not go on to estimate the monetary value of a working day lost, nor can one simply take the average daily working wage to do this. One reason for this is that employers are likely to have made *some* adjustment to their offered wage rates to reflect expectations about days not worked. Ostro's concern, however, is to supply an estimate of the morbidity elasticity.

iv) Dose-Response Approaches and Consumer Choice

Dose-response approaches are somewhat "mechanistic". It will be observed that none of the studies sets up any "model" of how consumers behave, although behavioural factors are present in some of the procedures used to put the money value on "life". Some researchers feel that this absence of a behavioural model renders dose-response studies unsatisfactory, and they have attempted to evolve a model of consumer choice which includes expenditures on health care which are designed to offset the effects of pollution. Notable studies are Cropper (1981) and Gerking and Stanley (1986).

Dose-response studies do not allow for the fact that medical services will be demanded by the individual as a "defensive" or "avertive" expenditure against pollution [a partial exception is the work of Crocker *et al.* (1979) in which the supply of doctors is related to the level of air pollution]. The "health capital" approach assumes that individuals choose a stock of health which in turn is determined positively by medical services, over which the individual has some control, and negatively by air pollution, over which the individual may have little or no control. In this way, the individual's welfare is partly a function of pollution – pollution affects health, and health is affected by medical services bought to offset the effects of pollution. A formal outline of such a model is given in Annex 7.

Gerking and Stanley (1986) use such a model to estimate the willingness to pay for reductions in air pollution in St Louis 1977-1980. They estimate the willingness to pay for a 30 per cent reduction in the mean ozone range from $18.45 to $24.48 per annum, which is about 60 per cent of the average cost of one visit to the doctor. The procedure estimates an equation linking medical care consumption to measures of air pollution, socioeconomic status and health status. Neither sulphur oxides nor TSP were generally significant in the resulting estimated equations, and this contrasts with the Ostro work. Ozone levels were significantly related to medical care consumption, a result which fits the initial findings of Lipfert.

Gerking and Stanley comment on the small size of the WTP result. They note various data problems, and the fact that a 30 per cent reduction in ozone is itself very small. Their work is perhaps more important because of the use of a model which has its foundations in behavioural responses to air pollution.

v) Conclusions on Air Pollution and Health

As data sets improve we can expect further refinements of the dose-response approach to estimating pollution health effects. But where some years ago the influential work of Lave and Seskin might be regarded as having produced some consensus, later work is ambiguous, some of it supporting the Lave and Seskin conclusions, some of it casting serious doubt on the relationships found, particularly for sulphur pollution, and some of it suggesting a very dramatic increase in the importance of particulate pollution as far as morbidity is concerned. Alternative models have only been sparsely developed and applied, but they are suggestive in terms of the role which pollution plays. Finally we note that the sophisticated epidemiological data required for such studies are very rarely available outside the United States, and therefore the applicability of this technique in other countries is likely to be rather limited. Attempts to define the statistical relationship between air pollution and mortality in the United Kingdom have not found a demonstratable connection [Chinn *et al.* (1981), Pickles (1986)].

5.3. MATERIALS CORROSION

i) Introduction

Air pollution affects exposed surfaces and causes corrosion of metals and deterioration of building surfaces. The fundamental problem of benefit estimation in this context is not the determination of the economic parameters, although the procedures for estimating them are not straightforward if a very detailed assessment is required. The difficulty lies in the physical data, notably in estimating the dose-response relationship and then in estimating the quantity of material that is at risk.

It is as well to distinguish between materials which are part of the standard housing stock, or part of the stock of commercial buildings and infrastructure (e.g. bridges), and the stock of historic buildings and monuments which also suffer acid deposition. Essentially the indirect dose-response approach is relevant to the former, but not to the latter. Although it is possible to measure a dose-response relationship for historic buildings, the next stage of applying a measure of valuation to a "unit" of damage is not meaningful. Instead, it seems better to proceed by the direct route and seek preferences for time restoration of such monuments or buildings. The obvious methodology is the contingent valuation approach (CVM) although we know of no attempt to apply it to such man-created assets. The costs of restoration set a lower limit to willingness to pay if and only if preferences for restoration exceed these costs. The measurement of the preferences for restoration requires the estimation of user and existence values. User values for historic monuments could be estimated using the travel cost approach – see Chapter 4.5. Existence values are likely to be far more important, however, and these would require the use of CVM.

ii) Non-Unique Materials Damage

The pollutants most widely implicated in the materials damage are the sulphur compounds, particulate matter, oxidants and nitrogen oxides, and, of these, sulphur compounds and particulates tend to dominate most damage estimates. The materials damaged range form electrical contact and components, to paints, metals – especially zinc and steel – fibres, textiles, rubber and elastomers. Most of the quantative work on dose-response relationships has been on sulphur compounds – SO_2, H_2S, COS and sulphate particulates. Nitrogen oxides may, however, be important with respect to the corrosion of electrical contacts. The problems of securing dose-response relationships are indicated by the fact that damage done may: a) be subject to threshold levels of sulphur deposition on the relevant surfaces, and b) be subject to the influence of the microclimate, for example in determining humidity. Additionally, corrosion rates for steel are partly determined by the interaction of different pollutants.

For non-unique materials the state-of-the-arts approach is illustrated by a recent study by Horst *et al.* (1986). They estimate materials damage from air pollution in four United States cities – Cincinatti, New Haven, Pittsburgh and Portland. First they estimate a dose-response relationship relating rates of materials erosion to levels of SO_2, H^+. This relationship is then applied to an inventory of building materials, which has been constructed by taking a detailed sample of a particular tract and then extrapolating it to a wider area. From this the rates of loss of physical quantities of materials due to these forms of air pollution are obtained. Then, to estimate economic damages the following assumptions are made:

a) That in the presence of air pollution maintenance rates will be such as to keep buildings in the condition they would have with no air pollution;

b) That the materials used for this purpose are the same as those currently being used and are to be valued at their current market prices; and

c) That the labour required for the maintenance is to be valued at its current market wage.

The figures obtained in this way are taken to be an estimate of the damage done by the current levels of air pollution in these four cities. As an extension of the same study the methodology is also applied to 113 United States cities in the North East quadrant of the country. The basis of this extrapolation is an estimated inventory of buildings and materials in the wider area, based on the more detailed inventories for the four cities cited above.

The use of current prices and wages seems reasonable in the case of air pollution damage, but difficulties arise with regard to *a)* and *b)*. First, it is being assumed that no mitigative behaviour is being undertaken. Principally this would involve the use of pollution resistent materials in the areas of high pollution, and since these would only be employed if they were cheaper than using regular materials and undertaking regular maintenance, the latter will tend to overestimate the costs of maintenance. On the other hand, the use of pollution resistant materials in manufacture or construction could lead to an underestimate of the materials costs. For example, as Horst *et al.* state, vinyl coated gutters are more expensive than galvanized gutters and more frequently used in high acid deposition areas. The costs associated with these are not included in calculations based solely on the materials used in the current inventory of buildings.

Second, it is being assumed that there is a fairly mechanical relationship between increases in air pollution and increases in the frequency of maintenance. In fact the relationship between these two variables can be quite complex. Take repainting as an example. The pollution causes erosion of the paint, but repainting decisions are based on factors such as peeling and cracking rather than erosion as such, and the former are not straightforwardly related to the latter. Hence using critical levels of erosion to determine increases in the frequency of repainting may be quite misleading. Furthermore, victims in polluted areas can simply leave paintwork to deteriorate more than they would in a pristine environment. In that event the costs of pollution are overestimated by assuming a constant level of maintenance.

On the labour side, uncertainty arises because the overall cost of labour depends very much on the quality of the repainting that is being done and who does it. This can range from cheap do-it-yourself jobs to professional work which would include surface preparation, scraping and sanding, and the application of two surface coats. However, there is not much evidence available on how much of each kind of painting is done on exterior surfaces.

The uncertainty in the physical damage function and in the costs of that damage are assessed by Horst *et al.* They find that, in the range of estimates obtained for each city, the top estimate can be 12 times as large as the bottom estimate. The main source of this uncertainty appears to be paint costs, and it is the relative importance of these that determines the size of the range for each city.

The Horst *et al.* study was subject to a detailed review by the EPA. This concluded that, although the study was well done, given the limitations of the data, the uncertainty inherent in the physical and economic relationships made the results unsuitable for the determination of policy in this area. The main sources of this uncertainty were identified as the physical damage functions relating paint and mortar erosion to the levels of SO_2 and H^+. In addition, the points made above regarding the economic damage calculations were also mentioned. However, the review concluded that the methodology was worth developing and that the estimates obtained would be improved as further scientific and behavioural data are collected.

iii) Some Aggregate Estimates

At the aggregate level some figures are available for Europe as a whole, for Netherlands and Germany

separately, and for the United States. We consider each of these in turn, converted, for ease of comparison, into 1983 dollars. For Europe, the information on dose-response function has been conveniently assembled by The economic Commission for Europe (Geneva 1982). This provides broad relationships for sulphur compounds and their impacts on carbon steel, zinc and galvanized steel, nickel and nickel-plated steel, copper materials and aluminium. The available evidence for damage to sandstone and limestone is given. The nature of damages to painted surfaces is not known with any precision and the ECE team report that even less is known about the damage to plastics and rubber. After reviewing various economic assessments of material damage, the ECE team conclude that sulphur compound damage to materials other than historic buildings is of the order of $3-14 per capita per annum in 1983 dollars. This overall figure may be compared with that of the Netherlands and Germany. In the Netherlands, materials damage from air pollution, excluding some restoration expenses, was estimated at $8-15 per capita per annum in 1983 dollars (Netherlands Ministry of Housing and Environment-1986. In Germany, materials damage to buildings and steel structures, but excluding monuments, was estimated by Heinz (1986) to be around $15 per capita per annum in 1983 dollars. Finally, for the United States, Freeman (1982) obtained a figure of about $28. This includes material damage from sulphur compounds, NO_x and oxidants.

iv) Conclusion

This brief discussion indicates the complexity of securing damage estimates for materials. Several important sources of materials damage are yet to be quantified. These include damage to concrete structures, automobiles, electrical components and plastics and rubber. Where the dose-response relationships are capable of estimation, it is evident that the relevant coefficients are subject to wide ranges and will vary from region to region. Furthermore, in obtaining aggregate demand estimates, there are serious problems of obtaining an accurate inventory of the materials that are exposed to air pollution. In spite of the difficulties, however, progress is being made on the scientific and statistical fronts, and the numbers that we have at present, should be improved in the near future.

5.4. VEGETATION DAMAGE

i) Dose-Response Relationship

The impact of air pollution on crops is well documented, and a considerable amount of research has been undertaken to place an economic value on the damage done by such forms of pollution as increased ozone concentrations on agricultural products. Some work has also been done on the impact of acid rain deposition on agricultural products. Ozone concentrations have an adverse effect on the crop yields of soyabeans, wheat, corn, cotton, sugar beets and fresh vegetables. In the United States a major investigation of this relationship at an experimental level has been undertaken by the EPA under the National Crop Loss Assessment Network (NCLAN) programme. As a result of this and other work, our knowledge of the dose-response relationship has improved considerably. Although there are still some areas of uncertainty, particularly with regard to the interaction of ozone with other pollutants and the interaction of ozone levels and moisture stress, the scientific data are accurate enough to allow us to make some useful economic cost calculations. Acid rain deposition has also been found to have a detrimental effects on the yields of soyabeans. The data on this form of pollution, however, are not as secure as that of ozone pollution, and the mechanisms behind the productivity declines have not been agreed upon.

Forests in Europe and North America are endangered and damaged. Air pollutants are an essential cause of forest damage. Conversion processes during the transport of pollutants in the air play an important role. This concerns the formation of photo oxidants, in particular of ozone, as well as the formation of strong acids as a result of a further oxidization of SO_2 into SO_4. Recent experiments have also shown significant reactions to the impact of combinations of pollutants such as ozone, SO_2 and NO_2 with a synergistic effect. The conditions for the formation of these secondary products improve with increasing distance from the emitting source. Needle and leaf loss as well as yellowing lead to a dangerous state of weakening forests and may cause a decrease in forest productivity, and to some extent the death of trees.

ii) Economic Valuation

Given the scientific data relating measures of air pollution to reductions in crop yields, the economic valuation of that reduction can take place at varying levels of sophistication. The simplest procedure is to multiply the reduction in output attributable to the pollutant by the current price of that output. Such a calculation is of course only valid even as an approximation even if the price that prevails is a market clearing one. If the price is set administratively at above the market clearing level, as is the case for a number of agricultural products, then the value of the increased output is less clear. It could be used to reduce the support price to the producer while still maintaining the same level of support, but the value of this cannot be measured without recourse to information on the full market structure. Given then that we are dealing with a market

clearing situation, the market value of the increased output is still only an approximation to the true value of the reduction in pollution because it takes no account of the fact that producers will have adjusted their behaviour to the higher pollution levels and the impact of that pollution will thereby have been mitigated. This adjustment in behaviour can be brought about by growing more of the varieties whose yields are resistant to the particular forms of air pollution in the region – e.g. it is known that rape covers its sulphuric requirements from acid rain deposition. By altering the use of other inputs such as calcium carbonate the impact of pollution can be minimised.

In order to predict what would be the *status quo* if the pollution level were to be reduced, a model of producer behaviour at different levels of air quality is required. The model that economists use in this context is one were the agricultural producer is taken to be a maximiser of expected profits, who takes as given the prices of all inputs and outputs. Then, given the production technology and the yield response relationship, we can derive the supply curves for each of the varieties of crops produced in a region. These supply relationships have been estimated on the assumption of this profit-maximising model and found to fit well to the actual data. They specify the amount that will be supplied of each crop as a function of the prices of all the crops, the prices of the variable inputs, the quantities of the fixed inputs, and the level of air pollution. Hence, if the pollution levels were to fall, the supply of products that were adversely affected by that pollution would be expected to increase and the output of those products whose yields were pollution resistant to decrease. The impact of these supply changes on the prices of the commodities will depend on the market structure that is prevalent. Again, if the prices are market determined, they will adjust to bring supply and demand into balance, and the magnitude of the price change will depend upon how many producers are affected by the pollution and how responsive supply and demand are to price changes. If, on the other hand, the prices are administratively set, then there is no direct price effect to consider. However, the prices of related commodities that are market determined may be affected.

The upshot of all this is that, in order to assess the impact of a change in something like ozone concentrations or acid deposition, a model of the markets for the products affected is required, in which specific account is taken of the yield response relationship of the supply side and of the impact of prices on the demand side. Given such a model one can calculate the pre and post pollution prices and quantities for each commodity. The change in the sum of the consumer surpluses plus the change in the profits of the producers, less any increase in government subsidies, is then regarded as an approximation to the economic benefits of the change in pollution levels. Modelling such an interrelated system of markets is an open ended activity and can be extremely sophisticated or fairly simple.

One point to note is that the crude measure that this analysis started with, where the percentage change in yield is multiplied by the price, is, for the market clearing case, an upper limit to the economic benefits of a reduction in pollution. This is because it ignores any adjustments incorporated in the status quo on account of the pollution. Since it is relatively easily calculated, it is well worth obtaining this upper limit, in the case where the products affected have market determined prices. A related question that then arises is, how far is this upper limit from the true value? In a study of the economic impact of ozone damage on selected crops in Southern California, Adams, Crocker and Thanavibulchai (1982) found that the crude estimate was about 20 per cent higher than the estimate obtained by modelling the supply and demand responses in a fairly sophisticated way. While this may be a significant error, it is probably smaller than the errors arising from other sources. For example, in a more recent study of ozone pollution impact on agricultural output in the corn belt of the United States, Adams and McCarl (1985) find that variation in the varieties selected for use in the assessment can cause the estimated benefits to vary by as much as 112 per cent compared to the "best" estimate; that changes in the response model specification can result in variations of around 73 per cent; and that alternative specifications of the ozone-moisture stress relationship can cause variations of around 50 per cent on either side of the best estimate. Adams and McCarl suggest that these ranges may in fact be too large, but they are, nevertheless, indicative of the kind of accuracy that one can hope for from these models. Moreover the kinds of improvements that can be expected to be obtained on the scientific information rapidly run into diminishing returns as far as the range of economic benefits is concerned. This has been demonstrated by Adams, Crocker and Katz (1984).

iii) Some Results

The sorts of numbers that emerge from the studies of vegetation damage suggest that the benefits of a 33 per cent reduction in ozone concentrations from 12 ppm (the current United States standard) to 8 ppm, are around 3 per cent of the value of farm output in the affected areas. This figure could be as low as 1.7 per cent and as high as 5.8 per cent. On the other hand increases in ozone concentrations of 50 per cent from present levels imply damages in the range of 3.8 per cent to 17.5 per cent [Adams and McCarl (1985)]. These figures are broadly in agreement with those obtained by Kopp, Vaughan and Hazilla (1984). Another study, which does not aggregate the benefits of ozone reduction across producers but models the economic impact at the farm level more fully, finds that this economic impact increases at an increasing rate as the ozone concentration rises [Garcia, Dixon and Mjelde (1986)].

The effects of acid deposition are more speculative. Adams, Callaway and McCarl (1986) used a model similar to that used by Adams and McCarl in the ozone study to value the damage done by acid rain to soyabean production. They found that a 50 per cent reduction in wet acid deposition resulted in damages of around US $140 000 in 1980 prices to United States agriculture. This represents a tiny percentage of the value of soyabean production (about 0.5). These figures are lower than some previous estimates and are probably the most reliable ones currently available. On the basis of the crude model outlined earlier, some North American and European national level damage estimates have been derived. We review their numbers below, along with some European national estimates of agricultural damage from air pollution, but we feel that further scientific work is required.

National level calculations of forest and agricultural damage have been attempted in Germany, the Netherlands, Canada and the United States. For Germany, Wicke (1986) has estimated agricultural damages from air pollution of not less than DM 1 billion per annum ($6 per capita in 1986 prices). Also Ewers *et al.* (1986) have estimated forestry damages (capital and recurrent) at DM 2.3 billion per annum and the cost of protective measures for the forestry sector at DM 630 million per annum. Altogether the latter two figures amount to about $17 per capita per annum in 1984 dollars. For the Netherlands it has been estimated [Netherlands Ministry of Housing and Environment (1986)] that overall damage to cultivated crops and heather regions has been running, since 1982, at between Gld 580-688 million per annum. In 1984 dollars this amounts to $13-15 per capita per annum. In addition, yield reductions on forestry were estimated at between Gld 20-50 million and the annual capital loss at between Gld 150-500 million. Together this amounts to $3-13 per capita per annum. For the United States, Crocker (1985) has estimated forest damage in the Eastern United States at $1.75 billion in 1978 dollars, and for Eastern Canada, Crocker and Forster (1985) estimate it as $CAN 1.5 billion. In per capita terms and in 1984 US dollars these figures amount to $7 and $46 respectively.

iv) Conclusion

The estimation of the effects of ozone levels on crops has now become quite well established, and the cost ranges obtained in these studies are both reliable and useful. We believe that more estimates of these costs are required, particularly outside the United States on the acid deposition question, the scientific parameters for crops are still not satisfactory, and, although estimates of damage have been obtained and quoted we feel that more scientific studies are required. As far as forest damage is concerned it must be maintained that many scientists have found evidence showing clearly that air pollution is an essential cause.

5.5. HOUSEHOLD SOILING

Air pollution, notably from particulate matter affects household cleaning. Watson and Jaksch (1982) have estimated household welfare losses arising from increased cleaning of walls and windows and increased painting of surfaces. Their national estimates for the United States are as follows:

Improvement in existing TSP to ($\mu g/m^3$)	Benefit (1971 \$) 10^6
100	613
75	1 547
60	2 656
55	3 167

They argue that these benefits may well outweigh other national benefit components, indicating the importance of estimating soiling damage.

Chapter 6

SELECTED PROBLEMS IN BENEFIT ESTIMATION

6.1. INTRODUCTION

This chapter looks at some topics related to benefit estimation which often give particular cause for concern. How, for example, can benefit estimation deal with irreversible damage to unique assets? Once an asset is lost it is lost for ever and no amount of money can bring it back again. But the issue of compensating for such losses is still meaningful, so that benefit estimation is still relevant. Such losses also raise the issue of our obligations, if any, to future generations. Irreversible losses are losses to both to ourselves and our children, grandchildren and so on. Discount rates play a significant role in determining whether or not damage to future generations" interests and preferences matters very much. Some authors argue that the discount rates used to appraise environmentally benign investments should be lower than for other investments, so as to increase the weight attached to future benefits. Others argue that manipulation of the discount rate is not a proper way of accounting for the interests of future generations. They suggest that what weight we give to the future is an issue of choosing the "rules of the game" within which the choice of a discount rate is then important but secondary [Page (1986)]. At a practical level, however, there may be more chance of persuading analysts and decision-makers that lower discount rates are more suitable mechanisms for dealing with distant future damage than through a wholesale rethinking of the objective function that society uses to allocate resources between the present and the future. The debate on this issue is a familiar one, but it has only just started in earnest in terms of analytical approaches.

Two issues are addressed in this Chapter: irreversibility and discount rates.

6.2. THE RATE OF DISCOUNT

i) Reasons for a Rate of Discount

In both public and private decisions, benefits and costs occurring at different points in time are regarded as having different values simply because they occur at different times. The discount rate quantifies this effect of time on value. Thus a project generating a benefit of £1.10 in one year's time will be regarded as being of less value than one yielding £1.10 today, purely because it occurs a year later. The percentage by which the later return is reduced to obtain its value today is called the discount factor. The longer the interval between the two time periods, the greater the discount factor.

In private market transactions a discount factor arises for two reasons: the productivity of capital and the preference of individuals for present over future consumption. If a person is able to acquire a stock of machinery or a quantity of a renewable or growing resource such as a tree or some seed corn, he can expect over time to end up with more in value than he started with. This productivity of capital – both natural and man made – means that the producer is able to pay interest to anyone willing to lend him the money to acquire the capital resources in the first place. The interest payable renders his future income less valuable to him than his present income and accounts for discounting on the producer's side. On the consumer side, common experience suggests that individuals cannot generally be persuaded to lend money unless there is a positive real return to doing so. Other things being equal, they would prefer to consume a unit today than to have to postpone consumption for a year. Hence they naturally discount future consumption as being less valuable than present consumption. The combination of producers willing to borrow at positive rates of interest and consumers willing to lend at such rates determines a market rate of interest at which supply and demand are brought into balance. If this interest rate were, say 5 per cent per annum, then in private markets the marginal borrower and the marginal lender could be said to value a unit of income in one year's time at approximately 95 per cent of its value today and a unit of income in 14 years time at about 50 per cent of its present value. As a rule of thumb, dividing 70 by the rate of interest gives the number of years it takes for the future value to be half the present value.

ii) Issues in the Determination of the Discount Rate

This rather simplistic sketch of how interest rates are determined and how discounting arises ignores a number of complications. Tax rates on capital act to drive a wedge between time preference and productivity discount rates. The greater riskiness of some ventures relative to others means that lenders will use higher discount rates for riskier projects and so a range of such rates will be observed. Consumers as well as producers borrow money to even out consumption when income is unevenly spread. Finally monetary and fiscal policy is used by governments to control economic activity at a macroeconomic level, and this can influence short-term interest rates. In spite of all these complications, however, discount rates related to individual time preference and productivity of capital will be used by individuals contemplating inter-temporal transactions.

Since the discounting procedure brings all future costs and benefits into comparable units, discounted costs and benefits can be added together to give an overall net benefit figure. This net benefit is referred to as the discounted present value and, from the point of view of decision-making, provides a rule which can be used to allocate scarce funds. It should be noted that the higher the discount factor, the greater the weight given to costs and benefits occurring closer to the present and the smaller the weight given to items in the distant future. This is discussed in more detail when looking at how discounting affects the role given to the potentially large, but extremely distant, environmental costs of present-day investment projects.

So far a rationale has been provided for why discounting exists in private inter-temporal decisions, but this does not mean that discounting is socially justified. As far as the balance between the present and future generations is concerned, discounting gives less importance to the former. For example, if a fixed asset were to be divided between several generations and we chose to use it in such a way that the discounted present value of consumption were to be maximised, then the optimal decision could be to use it all in the first generation. Looked at this way it is not surprising that the economist, Ramsay, described discounting as "immoral" and another economist, Pigou, attributed it to a "defective telescopic faculty".

This unfairness of discounting is mitigated by two factors. The first comes into force if, instead of maximising the discounted present value of consumption, the maximand is the discounted present value of the *utility* or welfare that this consumption generates. If this utility increases at a decreasing rate, as seems reasonable, then some asset will be provided for future generations, but not as much as is provided for the present. Although in most applications it is not the discounted present value of utility that is being valued but that of consumption, utility does come into play in an indirect way. It does so through the prices attached to future quantities consumed. In the above example if we were to allow the price of future consumption to depend on the quantity available, then this would act in much the same way as taking utility does, because a smaller quantity being available means that its price, which is influenced by its marginal utility, would be higher.

The second factor in favour of discounting is that capital is in fact productive, and that the analogy of a fixed asset is invalid. If one thought of it as, say, a bag of seed corn then it can be seen that maximising the discounted present value of consumption (taking account of inter-temporal price variations) is not so unfair to future generations. Indeed it can work out the other way. If the productivity growth is high enough, and the planning period infinite, then the present value criterion can imply that all generations be kept at a subsistence minimum and society prepare for a huge splurge that never takes place! With the discount rate equal to the rate of productivity growth, however the criterion should yield an outcome that is both inter-temporally fair and efficient.

In a riskless economy with no capital taxes and the optimal levels of savings and investment, the marginal productivity of capital and the rate of time preference are equalised. Optimality here means a rate of investment that is in accordance with the maximisation of an inter-temporal welfare function that discounts the welfare of future generations at the rate of time preference. In practice, however, this ideal is not realised. Myopia in individual preference results in a free market allocating too little to investment and in a discount rate that is too high. This is one reason why the social rate of discount should be below the market rate. There are other reasons as well. With inadequate savings the social rate of time preference will be below the marginal productivity of capital. In that case, which rate should one use for discounting future costs and benefits? The issue is complicated and it is not appropriate to elaborate on it here, but in principle the choice of discount rate (which may be either of the above or a combination of them) will hinge on how the project is financed. The aim is to calculate the opportunity cost of capital. In so far as the projects are financed out of savings, the opportunity cost is the marginal productivity of capital, and, in so far as they are financed out of reduced consumption, it is the social rate of time preference.

A similar issue arises when taxes on capital result in the borrower's rate of interest (equalling the marginal product of capital) being greater than the lender's rate of interest (equalling the personal rate of time preference). The presence of risk also raises some issues. If the project is being undertaken by the public sector then the risk is being borne by all the taxpayers. Thus in public projects the risk is spread over a much larger population and this has led to the suggestion that in public projects financed through general taxation the risk premium should be practically excluded from the discount rate.

iii)   The Discount Rate and the Environment

From an environmental point of view the impact of discounting is twofold: on the one hand it increases the current rate of exploitation of natural resources, both renewable and non-renewable, and on the other hand it reduces the role given to environmental damages incurred in the future as a result of investment decisions taken today.

As far as natural resources are concerned, conservationists fear that private rates of discount are too high and can result in too rapid a rate of depletion for these resources. For non-renewable resources this could imply rapidly rising prices and scarcities in the future. For renewable resources such as fish and forests, too high a rate of discount can, in certain circumstances, result in the resource becoming extinct. The problem is exacerbated when the resource in question is a common property resource. The circumstances that give rise to extinction are not fully understood and certainly discounting per se does not imply extinction in either private or commonly owned resources. Nevertheless the mere possibility of exhaustion is a matter of serious concern and has led some economists to argue that such resources should be used only on a sustainable yield basis. Such a requirement would not normally conflict with an exploitation rule based on the maximisation of discounted present value returns from the resource, but if it did, then the imposition of the requirement of sustainability seems to be an attractive notion. For a fuller discussion of the difficult moral and economic problems involved in the choice of a discount rate in these circumstances, the reader is referred to Page (1977).

The effect of discounting on projects with potentially high environmental damage costs is a related issue. If a resource becomes extinct, it is unavailable to all future generations, and the value to be placed on this could be substantial. This question is more fully addressed in the context of irreversibilty in the next section.

iv) Conclusion

Overall, the question of discounting and the choice of the appropriate rate of discount to be used in public projects presents some of the most difficult moral and economic issues in the domain of social choice. The need for some discounting is generally accepted but, for environmentally sensitive projects further constraints on the available courses of action should be given serious consideration. Indeed our personal preference would be to use a unified discount rate for the valuation of all regulatory and investment decisions, including environmental ones. Where the latter have a particularly sensitive inter-temporal role, this should be accommodated by imposing a requirement that, whatever course of action is followed, a certain minimum availability of crucial environmental stock will be maintained.

6.3. IRREVERSIBILITY

i) Introduction

The costs associated with a large number of decisions are irreversible. A valley that is flooded for a hydroelectric dam cannot be restored to its original state. Ancient buildings that are pulled down for a road development may be reproducible if dismantled and moved, but invariably are lost forever. Radioactive waste, once produced, cannot be destroyed. It must be stored somewhere, and no storage option is without risk. That risk is then present for at least hundreds of years and maybe more. Clearly, any policy of not developing a valley, of not building the road, and of not building nuclear power stations involves a foregone benefit. The damage avoided by not taking a development decision has to be weighed against the benefits that the development would have conferred. But the "no development" decision at least leaves the option to develop at a later stage, whereas the development decision leaves no option to reverse irreversible damage. One approach which goes some way towards building these problems into a benefit-cost methodology has been developed by Krutilla and Fisher (1975) and conveniently extended and formalised by Porter (1982). We outline the basic ideas below. A formal model of the Krutilla-Fisher-Porter approach is given in Annex 8.

ii) The Krutilla-Fisher-Porter Model

Consider a valley containing unique natural assets and for which a hydroelectric development is proposed. Such a proposal was mooted for part of the Gordon river in Tasmania, Australia, in the late 1970s, but the area to be flooded included areas of great natural beauty and of anthropological interest, together with a religious significance for aborigines. In 1976 the World Wildlife Fund urged Australia to protect the ecosystems of South West Tasmania. Thus, once flooded, this wilderness area would be lost forever and the wilderness benefits would be lost. Whatever the benefits of hydroelectricity generation, then, these foregone benefits must be counted as part of the costs of the development. The net benefits of development could thus be written:

$$\text{Net Benefits} = B(D) - C(D) - B(P)$$

where $B(D)$ are the benefits of development, $C(D)$ are the development costs, and $B(P)$ are the net benefits of preservation (i.e. net of any preservation costs which are likely to be positive, i.e. the damage costs). All the benefit and costs items need to be expressed in present value terms, i.e. they need to be discounted. As noted above, some would argue that the discount rate itself should be set very low for projects with long-term environmental benefits or costs. In this case it would have the effect of making $B(P)$ large because they are foregone for ever, whereas the net benefits of development will be dissipated once the life of the dam is finished – perhaps 50 years after its construction. In the Krutilla-Fisher approach, however, the discount rate is "conventional" in that it is set equal to some measure of the marginal productivity of capital. We therefore proceed on this assumption.

The next thing to consider is that the benefits of preserving the area are likely to increase with time relative to other benefits in the economy. The reasons for thinking this are that *a)* the overall supply of natural wilderness is decreasing in every country in the world, *b)* the demand for "wilderness experience" tends to be increasing with income growth and with population growth which generates "crowding" effects, and *c)* the demand for wilderness to remain in its natural state even without it being directly experienced also appears to be growing (i.e. we surmise that existence values are increasing). The net effect is to raise the "price" of the wilderness asset through time. In a cost-benefit analysis, this is simply included by allowing benefits to increase at some rate of demand growth, say g. The net effect of letting preservation benefits grow at g per cent per annum and then discounting them back again at the discount rate of r per cent is to discount the benefits by a rate (r-g) per cent. In other words, the effect is very similar to using a lower discount rate for preservation benefits. In this sense, the Krutilla-Fisher approach is not markedly different to manipulating the discount rate, but it does preserve the use of a "conventional" discount rate which has the attraction that the procedure cannot be criticised for distorting resource allocation in the economy by using variable discount rates.

Krutilla and Fisher engage in a similar adjustment for development benefits, but in reverse. They argue that technological change will tend to reduce the benefits from developments such as hydroelectricity which will be reduced because superior electricity generating technologies will take their place over time. The example quoted in their work is nuclear power. Clearly, the empirical relevance of this argument can now be disputed, but it is useful to develop the analysis on the assumption that development benefits will be subject to this technological depreciation. Let this rate of depreciation be k per cent per annum. The effect is to produce a net discount rate on development benefits of (r + k) per cent. That is, the discount rate applied to development benefits has increased.

This, in essence, is the basis of the Krutilla-Fisher approach. It is in fact far more complicated than this because it is extended to allow for limits to the rate of growth of preservation benefits, ways of estimating the rate of technological change, and an analysis of the benefits and costs of postponing decisions so that further information about the gains and losses can be obtained. The important point, however, is that the procedure does not in fact require that benefits be estimated. Instead, the procedure is to calculate the net benefits of development – i.e. the value of the output of electricity minus associated costs – and then to ask what the value of preservation benefits *would have to be* for the development not to take place. As a check, however, it should be possible to estimate *user* benefits by adopting the travel cost method of recreational benefit analysis. On a grander scale, the contingent valuation method could be used to obtain preservation benefits overall. These could then be compared directly with the development benefits.

iii) Application to the Gordon River Dam in Tasmania

The Krutilla-Fisher approach was used by Saddler, Bennett, Reynolds and Smith (1980) in their evaluation of the proposed Gordon River hydroelectricity development. They report various results according to different assumptions about the rate of growth of preservation benefits and different discount rates. With a discount rate of 5 per cent, a value for g = 4 per cent, and an assumed capacity to absorb visitors such that g applies only for 30 years, Saddler and his colleagues obtain the following result: $ 1 of preservation benefits in the initial year will have a present value of $A 260. (*Note*: there are additional parameter values relevant to this calculation. It is not a simple matter of summing the discounted value of $A 1 each year for 30 years.) Now, Saddler *et al.* estimate that the hydroelectric option would be cheaper than an alternative coal-fired option for generating electricity. The difference between the two is a present value of cost savings of $A1 89 million. Dividing the $A1 89 million by $A 260 gives some $ 725 000. What this means is that if the preservation benefits are $ 725 000 in the first year, then the present value of preservation benefits will exceed the difference in the cost of the coal-fired and hydroelectric schemes. Expressed differently, the preservation benefits outweigh the cost differential, and hence they justify the adoption of the more expensive electricity generation scheme (coal) which does not involve the destruction of the wilderness area. The only issue remaining, then, is to ask whether the preservation benefits are likely to be $A 725 000 in the first year. The answer could be judgmental – i.e. simply letting decision-makers decide if this is below what they think the first year preservation benefits are. Or user benefits could be estimated on a travel cost basis. Or total preservation benefits could be estimates using the CVM approach. In the Saddler *et al.* study the result is left to judgement, and for a unique wilderness area it is more than unlikely that preservation values lie below this figure.

The Gordon dam was never built, in large part because of the worldwide outcry against the proposal. This example illustrates the way in which benefit estimation is not always needed to gain considerable insight into the costs and benefits involved in a development proposal that has major environmental consequences. On the other hand, it is also significant that a benefit estimate might help to "clinch" the analysis. For example, while in this case it is self-evident that preservation benefits are larger than the minimum required amount, it is perfectly possible to imagine cases where the analysis would not be so clear cut.

Chapter 7

CONCLUSIONS AND SUMMARY

7.1. INTRODUCTION:
THE USES OF MONETARY BENEFIT ESTIMATION

Monetary benefit estimates attempt to measure the value which individuals place on environmental damage or benefit. The usual presumption in benefit analysis is that the individuals in question are the population at large. It could be that benefit estimates are judged "paternally" by decision-makers themselves, and it was shown in Chapter 2 that monetary values of benefits are always *implied*, whether we are conscious of the process or not.

In this overview of benefit estimation techniques, uses and results, however, we have assumed that the measures in question always relate to individuals at large.

This basic observation serves to underline one very important limitation of monetary benefit estimation: it is usable only when the relevant criterion for making a judgement on policy is what people want. If the basis is some other objective – fairness, national security, a paternal overriding of individual preferences because of the "merit good" aspect – then benefit estimation of the kind discussed here is not immediately relevant to decision-making.

Even in such contexts, however, a failure to consider benefit estimates (if they can be made) is unwise. Essentially this is because the measurement of benefits relates to the concept of economic efficiency, of finding improvements in social welfare at minimum cost in terms of resources. It follows that, if benefit estimates are to be ignored totally, the onus is on the decision-maker to explain why economic efficiency is not a relevant consideration. Alternatively, it may be the case that the argument about economic efficiency is accepted, but it is judged that monetary benefit estimates are not reliable indicators of individuals' preferences. That is a judgement about the accuracy of benefit estimation. To make that judgement it is necessary to have some familiarity with the ways in which the estimates are made. That has been the purpose of this volume.

To summarise on the uses of benefit estimates, then, one might say:

i) Benefit estimates are relevant whenever economic efficiency is the objective, or one of the objectives, of environmental policy (Chapter 1);

ii) The use of benefit estimates is as reliable as the estimates themselves are reliable, in terms of measuring individual preferences. This is the subject of this volume;

iii) It is a matter of judgement as to how accurate the various benefit measurement techniques are;

iv) So-called "alternative" decision-making techniques are open to many of the criticisms of cost-benefit analysis, for which benefit estimation is essential (Chapter 2);

v) Other techniques also suffer in that they are not rigorously linked to economic efficiency as an objective, and some appear to have no well-defined criterion of importance at all;

vi) Other techniques may be preferred in terms of "transparency" of the measured impacts they use. Money benefit estimates often obscure the underlying assumptions and processes for deriving them;

vii) Other techniques may be preferred because they relate more clearly to objectives other than economic efficiency (Chapter 1).

7.2. THE APPLICATION OF BENEFIT TECHNIQUES

Which techniques are applicable to which problems? Rather than engage in extensive discussion, we offer our own assessment in terms of a matrix of environmental "sectors" and valuation techniques. This is shown in Table 15. We then consider each technique in terms of various criteria for use: data problems in the physical models underlying our understanding of the environmental sector in question, relationship to economic theory, the extent to which a benefit – *function* – as opposed to a point estimate of benefits can be achieved, reliability of measures obtained (which will be partly dependent upon the underlying physical model's reliability), the number of studies carried out (a crude

Table 15. **A matrix of benefit techniques by environmental sector**

Pollution	Type of effect	Benefit impact	Benefit estimation technique						Comment
			Hedonic property	Hedonic wages	Travel cost	Contingent valuation	Dose-response	Other techniques	
AIR POLLUTION									
1. Conventional pollutants (TSP, SO$_x$, NO$_x$)	Respiratory illness	WLD, RAD, medical expenses, suffering	O	L	O	X	X	Health capital model	
	Respiratory death	Death	L	X	O	O	X		Some wage valuation experience
	Aesthetics	Visual, sensory	X	L	O	X	O		
	Recreation	Visits especially to forests	O	O	X	X	O		
	Materials	Maintenance/repair	O	O	(?)	(?)	X		For historic monuments
	Vegetation	Crop losses	O		O	O	X		Forest reclamation
WATER POLLUTION									
1. Conventional pollutants (BOD, etc.)	Recreation: fishing, boating, etc.	Visit behaviour	L	O	X	X	O		
	Commercial fisheries	Stock losses	O	O	O	O	X		
	Aesthetics	Turbidity, odour, unsightliness	X	O	L	X	O		
	Ecosystem	Habitat and species loss	O	O	O	X	X		
2. Trace concentrations	Drinking water	Illness, mortality	O	O	O	(?)	X		
	Fisheries	Stock	O	O	O	O	X		
TOXIC SUBSTANCES									
1. Air (benzene, PCB, pesticides)	Illness and mortality	WLD, RAD, medical expenses, suffering(?)	X	O	X	X	X		
2. Hazardous chemicals to land	Aesthetics	Unsightliness	X	O	O	X	O		
	Ecosystem	Health, anxiety, ecosystem losses	O	O	O	X	X		
RADIATION	Illness, mortality,	WLD, RAD, lives lost	(?)	X	O	L	X		
MARINE POLLUTION									
Oil, radioactive substances, sewage	Aesthetics, swimming	Unsightliness, visit behaviour, illness, fish stock losses	(?)	O	X	X	X		
NOISE	Nuisance	Annoyance	X	O	O	X	L		

X = Used technique; (?) = Not developed but possible;
O = Non-usable technique; WLD = Work loss days;
L = Very limited application exists; RAD = Restricted activity days.

Table 16. **Assessment of benefit estimation techniques**

	Technique				
	Hedonic property prices	Hedonic wages	Travel cost	Contingent valuation	Dose-response/ damage cost
"Physical" data problems	No	Yes	Yes	No	Yes
Benefit function?	Yes	Yes	Yes	Yes	Assumed
Sophistication	High	High	High	High	High
Relation to Behavioural Theory	Yes	Yes	Yes	Yes	No
Problems	Sensitivity to model-specification			Hypothetical bias	Sensitivity to model-specification
	Free markets important		Travel time cost measurement		
			Influence of site substitutes	WTP/WTA disparity	
Special features	Main technique for workplace		Use limited to recreation	Can cover existence	Only method for many issues
	Can be cross-checked with contingent valuation			Only method for many issues	Requires separate valuation technique

indicator of the "sophistication" or the "research status" of the approach), and other selected observations. This is shown in Table 16.

A number of observations are in order:

i) The tables show that there are several alternative techniques available for use for most environment problem areas. This is an attractive feature because it allows us to test at least the consistency of the measures obtained. As the main text observed, one of the features of those comparisons that have so far been made is that they do tend to suggest a broad convergence of values. While this cannot demonstrate the "correctness" of any of the techniques, it is reassuring;

ii) Some of the techniques, notably the contingent valuation and dose-response approaches, have very wide coverage. This suggests in turn that the greatest research effort should be made for these techniques. We also suggest that current reliability is fairly high for these techniques, a judgement that has altered in light of the theoretical and empirical efforts that have been made in the last decade, and especially in the last 5-7 years;

iii) While we have attempted to survey European and other studies in this volume, it will be evident that the overwhelming research effort in benefit estimation has been confined to the United States. There are no ready explanations for this bias;

iv) While there are many problems to be solved, and many that perhaps can never be settled, the final issue is one of judging whether the kinds of results obtained in these studies are within a broadly acceptable range of acceptability. We judge that they are, and that further improvements can be expected in many areas.

OPTION PRICES

For contexts in which there is certainty about demand and supply, the proper valuation of a natural asset is given by the flow of consumer surplus (suitably discounted). In the context of *uncertain* demand and supply the option price literature indicates that consumer's surplus should not be the appropriate valuation. Instead, *option price* is the valuation required.

The literature indicates that

a) Under *demand uncertainty*, option price may be greater or less than the expected value of consumer's surplus;

b) Under – *supply uncertainty* –, option price will *tend* to be greater than expected consumer surplus.

i) Demand Uncertainty

For a given consumer there is assumed to be uncertainty about his future preferences for the good in question. Two possible states are: 1. that he will want the good and 2. that he will not want it. His utility function may be written as:

$$E = \sum_{i=1}^{i=2} \pi_i V^i(Y_i \, P_i) \tag{A1}$$

where π = probability that state i (i=1,2) will occur;

Y_i = income in state i;

P_i = price of all goods in state i;

V^i = an indirect utility function of income and prices.

When the good is available, it has a price of p*. When it is not available, we define it as having a price of P' which will be very high (if the good is wholly not available it will tend to infinity). Then:

$$V^i(Y_i, P') = V^i(Y_i - CS_i, P^*) \qquad i=1,2 \tag{A2}$$

where CSi is the consumer's willingness to pay to preserve the good. Equation (A2) states that utility in the state in which the good is (certain to be) not available (and hence P' prevails) is equal to the utility in the state where the good is certain to be available through the sacrifice of CS as the willingness to pay to preserve the good. For a diagrammatical exposition, see Pearce and Nash (1981, pp. 78-81).

To introduce option price, hypothetically reduce income in both states until the consumer is indifferent between buying an option to consume the good and not buying the option.

This is where:

$$\sum_{i=1}^{i=2} \pi_i V^i(Y_i - OP, P^*) = \sum_{i=1}^{i=2} \pi_i V^i(Y_i, P') \tag{A3}$$

where OP is now the option price. The LHS of equation (A3) gives us the expected utility across the two states given that the option is purchased at price OP and the actual price P* therefore prevails. The RHS of equation (A3) gives the expected utility across the two states given that the option is *not* purchased and hence Pi prevails.

We define option value, OV, as:

$$OV = OP - \sum_{i=1}^{i=2} \pi_i CS_i \tag{A4}$$

or, option value is the difference between option price and the expected value of consumer surplus. Substituting (A2) into (A3) gives:

$$\sum_{i=1}^{i=2} \pi_i V^i(Y_i - OP, P^*) = \sum_{i=1}^{i=2} \pi_i V^i(Y_i - CS, P^*) \tag{A5}$$

The conditions for concave functions dictate that:

$$V^i(Y_i - OP, P^*) \leqslant V^i(Y_i - CS_i, P^*) + [CS - OP]V^i_Y(Y_i - CS_i, P^*) \tag{A6}$$

where V^iY is $\delta V^i/\delta Y_i$ or the conditional marginal utility of income. Substituting (A6) into (A5) therefore gives:

$$\sum_{i=2} \pi_i \, V^i_Y(Y_i - CS_i, P^*) \, [CS - OP] \geqslant O \tag{A7}$$

If the marginal utilities of income are equal in the two states such that $V^1_Y(Y_1 - CS_1, P^*) = V^2_Y(Y_2 - CS_2, P^*)$ then (A7) reduces to:

$$OV = OP - \sum_{i=1}^{i=2} \pi_i CS_i \leqslant 0 \tag{A8}$$

This shows that OV is zero or negative. On the other hand if $V^1_Y(Y_1 - OP, P^*) = V^2_Y(Y_2 - OP, P^*)$ then it can be shown that OV is zero or positive.

ii) Supply Uncertainty

The results for demand uncertainty are due to Schmalensee (1972). Bishop (1982) has extended them to supply uncertainty. Continuing with the two states, state 1 now refers to the existence of the good and state 2 to its extinction. Income in the two states is assumed to be equal ($Y_1 = Y_2 = Y$) and, since we assume away demand uncertainty, $U_Y^1(Y, P^i) = U^2Y(Y, P^2) = U_Y(Y, P^i)$. The probabilities of states 1 and 2 are π_1 and π_2 respectively. Let E_o be the expected utility if the option is purchased and E_{No} the expected utility if the option is not purchased. P_1 and P_2 are the two price vectors, such that in P2 the price of the good in question is so high that the demand is zero. From the previous analysis we have:

$$V(Y - CS_1, P_1) = V(Y, P_2) \tag{A9}$$

$$E_O = V(Y - OP, P_1) \tag{A10}$$

$$E_{NO} = \pi_1 V(Y, P_1) + \pi_2 V(Y, P_2)$$
$$= \pi_1 V(Y, P_1) + \pi_2 V(Y, - CS_1, P_1) \tag{A11}$$

But we know that $E_o = E_{No}$ (this is how OP is defined). Hence:

$$V(Y - OP, P_1) = \pi_1 V(Y, P_1) + \pi_2 V(Y - CS_1, P_1) \tag{A12}$$

Dropping for convenience the P1 term, which is constant throughout, the concavity conditions give us:

$$V(Y) < V(Y - OP) + [OP]V_Y(Y - OP) \tag{A13}$$

and

$$V(Y - CS_1) < V(Y - OP) + [OP - CS_1]V_Y(Y - OP) \tag{A14}$$

Multiplying (A13) by π_1, (A14) by π_2 and substituting from (A12) gives:

$$0 < \pi_1[OP]V_Y(Y - OP) + \pi_2[OP - CS]V_Y(Y - OP) \tag{A15}$$

or

$$OV = OP - \pi_2 CS_1 > 0 \tag{A16}$$

Hence the option value is positive. Bishop (1982) correctly points out that this result depends on certain knowledge of money income in the two states and on the utility function being known.

Annex 2

THE THEORY OF HEDONIC PRICES

The first stage of the hedonic price approach is the estimation of an equation of the form

$$P_h = f(S_h, N_h, A_h, Q_h) \qquad (A17)$$

where P_h is the value of property h (or of a group of similar properties), S_h is a collection of site variables such as lot size, number of rooms, age of building, etc.; N_h is a collection of neighbourhood variables such as housing density, local taxes, crime rate, etc.; A_h is a collection of accessibility variables such as distance to the central business district, to shopping areas, sources of transport, etc.; and Q_h is the collection of environmental attributes of interest usually measured so that an increase in Q_h implies a higher level of pollution.

The functional form of f(.) is of great importance. If it is linear then property prices are affected by a constant amount per unit change in the dependent variables. If the form implies that the relationship between P_h and Q_h is *concave* then as Q_h increases so property prices fall at an increasing rate. On the other hand a *convex* relationship would imply the reverse. Log, semi-log, and inverse semi-log forms of (A17) imply a convex relationship. Exponential or quadratic forms allow for the possibility that the function is concave.

The coefficient of Q_h in a log linear form would give the elasticity of P_h with respect to Q_h. So it tells us that if Q_h increases by one per cent then P_h will decrease, in percentage terms, by the amount of the coefficient. In all other forms this elasticity depends upon the values of Q_h and P_h but with the log linear form it does not. Equation (A17) is usually estimated on cross section data and problems of multicollinearity and heteroskedasticity can be quite severe. Given that the equation has been satisfactorily estimated, the marginal willingness to pay for a reduction in Q_h is given by the partial derivative, $\delta P_h / \delta Q_h$. We call this w_h.

As the second stage of the hedonic exercise, w_h is regressed on the household characteristics such as income and family size and on the measures of pollution to obtain an inverse demand function:

$$w_h = g(H_h, Q_h) \qquad (A18)$$

where H_h is a collection of household characteristics. If supply considerations are believed to be important then a supply function is estimated simultaneously with (A18).

From (A18) the benefits of a reduction in pollution levels from Q_{h0} to Q_{h1} are given by B_{01} where:

$$B01 = \Sigma \int_{Q_{h1}}^{Q_{h0}} g(H_h, Q_h) dQ_h \qquad (A19)$$

HEDONIC WAGES IN THE THEORY OF THE LABOUR MARKET

The basic theory of hedonic wage models is outlined in Rosen (1979). Although hedonic price models had developed a rationale for why land rents should vary with the environmental attributes of a site, Rosen showed that real wages would also vary with the site attributes of the place of residence and work. Consider a community of individuals with identical preferences and productivities, but occupying locations with different attributes. They all face the same prices for all goods other than the rental of the site that they occupy. Spatial and market equilibrium requires that all individuals enjoy the same level of welfare and this is brought about by rents at more desirable locations being higher than at less desirable ones. If that were not so then the demand would be greater at the more favoured spots and this would result in rents being bid up there. This process also influences the *real wage* of the individual. Let us assume initially that there are no productivity effects arising from the choice of location. For example, if there is pollution there then it does not reduce his capacity to work by affecting his health, or increase his productivity by making higher output possible. In this case, as the environmental quality improves, so the real wage will fall. This follows from the fact that everyone's productivity is the same, and all the prices are the same, except that those living in more desirable locations will be paying a higher rent. If productivity depends on the site's attributes then it is not clear whether real wages will rise or fall with improvements in environmental quality. However, Rosen has shown that as long as earnings account for a sufficiently large share of total income the wage-environmental quality locus will still be negatively sloped.

Thus we can see that almost as a mirror image to the hedonic price approach, there is an hedonic wage approach in which real wages will depend, *inter alia*, on the environmental attributes. Figure A-1 plots a possible equilibrium schedule between environmental quality q and the real wage w. The slope of this schedule gives us the value of a small improvement in quality in terms of the reduction in the real wage that is acceptable to the individual who experiences this improvement in quality. In general this marginal value or "price" of environmental quality will not be constant for different levels of quality. Furthermore, with differences in tastes and incomes, the differences in wages between points such as A and B will *not* reflect the willingness to pay for the improvement in

Figure A-1

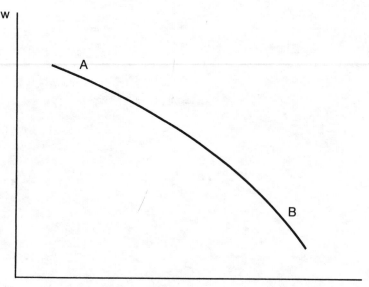

environmental quality of any one individual – a point which was also made earlier with regard to the interpretation of the hedonic price locus.

A careful application of the hedonic wage model is that of Smith (1983). He took data on wage rates for about 16 000 individuals and used cost of living measures for 44 Standard Metropolitan Statistical Areas in the United States to construct a real wage data set at the individual level. He then regressed this on: *a)* a number of *site specific variables* such as levels of air pollution, exposure to carcinogens, crime rates, unemployment rates and hours of sunshine; *b)* a number of – *individual specific variables* – such as the level of education, the years of experience, race and sex and; *c) job specific variables*, notably industrial injury rates and occupation. Smith found that individual and job specific variables performed as expected from previous studies which had looked at just those variables. The site specific variables that were consistently successful in explaining real wage differences were the cancer exposure index, the levels of total suspended particulates, the crime rate and the mean hours of sunshine. All these variables worked as shown in Figure A-1 – i.e. an improvement in environmental quality lowered the real wage.

The job specific variables of interest were the injury rate and the number of workers in each industry covered by collective agreements with provisions relating to health and safety conditions. The former was found to raise wages, as expected.

From this an implied annual value for an injury can be calculated, as explained in the text. The value obtained is similar to, though slightly lower than, that obtained from Viscusi's [1978(b)] study. (See Table 8 for details.) As far as the collective agreements are concerned, they were found to have a significant effect on real wages when multiplied by the cancer exposure index and the product used as a single variable. This implies that increasing participation in collective agreements does raise real wages, but it does so in greater measure if there is an increased danger present, as measured by the cancer exposure index. The purpose of including this variable is to pick up the effects of subjective knowledge or information about risk on the real wage differentials. Unfortunately this particular variable, the membership of workers in union organised collective agreements, picks up the union's bargaining strength as well, and so it is unclear what is being measured. It remains the case therefore that our understanding about this aspect of risk is very limited and further light on it is welcome.

Overall this study has shown that a number of the effects of environmental variables and work related risks affect real wages broadly as one would expect them to, and that the quantitative magnitude of these effects is consistent with other studies. Moreover the results are fairly robust under changes in the data set and under various checks made to test the validity of the specification.

RELATIONSHIP BETWEEN HEDONIC PRICES AND TRUE WILLINGNESS TO PAY

Brookshire *et al.* (1983) have demonstrated that rental differences due to reduced pollution will exceed willingness to pay for that improvement. This can be illustrated by using Figure A-2 shown below.

The vertical axis measures a composite consumption good, X, and also shows money values ($). The horizontal axis measures the level of pollution (P). I_0 is an indifference curve which shows the trade off between pollution and X – more of X is required to compensate for more P. Fix an arbitrary level of income Y_0. R is then the rental for sites with different levels of pollution and since R is greater the lower the level of pollution, the curve $Y_0 - R(P)$ will have the shape shown. The consumer's equilibrium is at A where X_0 is consumed, rental R_0 is paid and the pollution level is P_0.

What is the willingness to pay for a reduction in the level of pollution from P_0 to P_1, i.e. how much of X will the consumer be willing to give up for this reduction? The answer is W_0 since this is the reduction in X that the consumer will be prepared to make and still be as well off as he was on his original indifference curve I_0 with the combination (X_0, P_0). But the rental difference corresponding to this change in pollution level is ΔR, and $\Delta R > W_0$. ΔR is in fact the implicit price of pollution so that W_0, the true willingness to pay, is below the implicit or hedonic price R.

Figure A-2

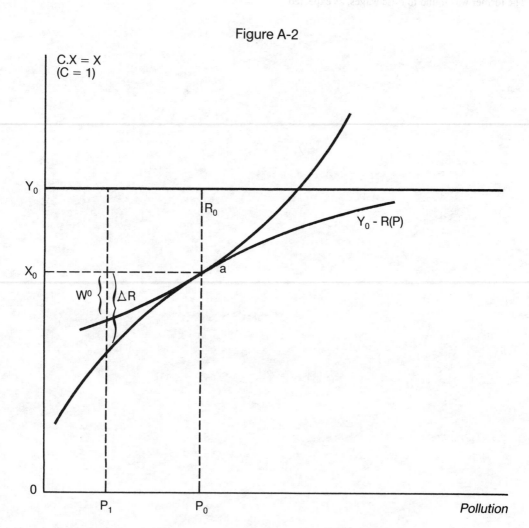

CONTINGENT VALUATION IN THE CONTEXT OF ECONOMIC THEORY

Consider a consumer whose preferences are represented by a utility function:

$$U = U(a_1, a_2, ... a_n; q_1, q_2, ... q_n; X) \qquad (A20)$$

This function is assumed to be quasi-concave in the "a"s and X. a_i is an activity level which is carried on in an environment of quality q_i. The higher the value of q_i, the better the environment. There are $\dot{n}$ such activities, and X is a composite commodity, representing all other goods and services. Quasi-concavity of the function implies that the indifference curves between any two of the "a"s or between any of the "a"s and X are convex to the origin in the usual fashion.

Define the expenditure of the consumer on the activities a_i and on X as E where:

$$E = \Sigma \ p_i a_i + X \qquad (A21)$$

p_i is the price of a unit of a_i and typically will depend on the levels of the environmental quality in that activity and in associated activities.

The *minimum* level of expenditure required to achieve a given utility level, U^0, will depend on what that level is, on the initial quality of the environment in each of the activities, and on the initial prices of the activities. Let this expenditure be m_0. If m_0 is set equal to the consumer's income Y, then this defines the initial equilibrium position for that consumer. This may be written as:

$$Y = m_0 = g(p_{10}, ... p_{n0}; q_{10}, ..., q_{n0}; U^0) \qquad (A22)$$

Consider an improvement in the environment on site 1 from q_{10} to $q11$ (i.e. $q_{11} > q_{10}$). The value of this improvement can be expressed in a number of ways. The situation is shown in Figure A-3 where m is plotted against q_1. Originally the consumer is at α and after the improvement he is at ß, which is

Figure A-3

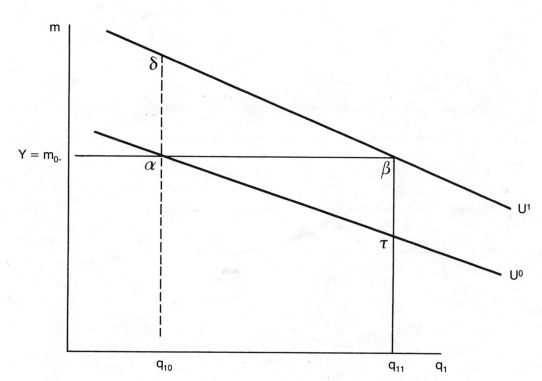

73

on a higher utility level than α. If his income were to drop from ß to τ, then he would be no worse off than he was before the change. Hence ß-τ is maximum willingness to pay for the improvement. This can be written as WTP_1:

$$WTP1 = g(p_{10},...p_{n0};q_{10},...q_{n0};U^0)$$
$$g(p_{10},...p_{n0};q_{11},...q_{n0};U^0) \qquad (A23)$$

Alternatively we can ask what he would be willing to accept for the improvement not to take place. If it did not take place, his income would have to increase from α to δ for him to be at least as well off. Hence δ-α is the minimum willingness to accept and can be written as WTA_1:

$$WTA_1 = g(p_{10},...p_{n0};q_{10},...q_{n0};U^1)$$
$$g(p_{10},...p_{n0};q_{11},...q_{n0};U^1) \qquad (A24)$$

As Section 4.4 (subsection v) indicates, where either the WTA or WTP is not significant relative to income, then theory would suggest that the two measures should not be too different. But theory and empirical evidence are not consistent, and the theory itself is now debated.

In CV method the question is designed to elicit either WTA or WTP. However, the way in which the question is framed is of great importance. The difficulty lies in what is assumed constant. If q_{10} changes to q_{11}, other variables of relevance may also change, or, equally importantly, be perceived to change. In so far as other prices will actually change, such changes should be allowed for when making the comparison. Often, however, these are not known accurately and this can result in errors of measurement. In addition errors can arise when the individual's perceptions of the change are incorrect. These will yield biases if the distribution of these perceptions has a mean that is different from the true value. For example, vehicle bias can arise if all individuals believe that along with the improvement the price of the activity will rise (p_1) or that their income will be reduced, *and* if these views are incorrect. If the price rises and income is reduced (perhaps because of general tax increases required to bring the improvement about) then the U^1 curve will be further out (higher p), and the point ß will be below the horizontal line extending from α. The combined impact of these two effects is not immediately obvious, but if one had information on the parameters of the underlying preferences, one might be able to evaluate the likely impact of particular kinds of vehicle and instrument bias. The same applies even more forcefully when many of the "p"s and other "q"s are perceived to change.

This representation shows how important it is both to clarify what is changing and what is not, and to make that classification credible. It also stresses that for biases to occur individuals must hold views about the impact of the change that systematically deviate from the actual outcome.

ANALYTICS OF TRAVEL COST MODELS

The underlying model of household behaviour specifies:

a) a household utility function as a function of the recreational services consumed (R) and of other goods (E). The utility level is written as U where:

$$U = U(R,E) \tag{A25}$$

b) a household "production function" which has as an output the level of recreational services of site i (R_i), and has as inputs the number of visits to the site (V_i), the time taken to make a visit to the site (T_i), and the recreational attributes of the site (A_i). This can be written formally as:

$$R_i = R(V_i,T_i,A_i) \tag{A26}$$

The household, visiting several sites, has a budget constraint:

$$Y = w.H + N + L = E + \sum_i (d_i+q.T_i).V_i \tag{A27}$$

It also has a time constraint:

$$T = H + \sum_i T_i.V_i \tag{A28}$$

The variables have the following interpretations:

Y   is the potential household income, or what it could earn if it worked all the hours available.
N   is the non wage income.
L   is the foregone income as a result of the recreational activities.
d_i is the monetary cost of travelling to and visiting the site.
q   is the opportunity cost of recreational travel time.

For simplicity we can define the "cost" of a visit to a site i as p_i where:

$$p_i = d_i + q.T_i \tag{A29}$$

The household maximises (A25) subject to (A26) – (A27) and the identity linking R_i to R:

$$R = \sum_i R_i \tag{A30}$$

The maximisation yields a demand function for R which can be written as:

$$R = R(p_1,p_2,....p_i,...;Y) \tag{A31}$$

Our aim is to obtain a set of equations for V_i that we can estimate, given this overall demand function for recreational services. In order to do this we need to make some simplifying assumptions. The first is that in (A26) the relationship

between R_i and V_i is strictly increasing. Then we can invert (A26) to obtain:

$$V_i = V_i(T_i,A_i,R_i) \tag{A32}$$

The next assumption is that V_i is separable into two sub functions, one of which depends only on T_i and A_i and the other depends only on A_i.i.e:

$$V_i = G(T_i,R_i).H(A_i) \tag{A33}$$

Equation (A33) states that each site's services can be transferred into units $H(A_i)$ which are then comparable across sites. Both the functions $G(.,.)$ and $H(.)$ are site independent. If the relationship between visits and attributes is as given above then an equal outlay on two sites i and j will result in visits V_i and V_j such that:

$$V_i/V_j = H(A_i)/H(A_j) \tag{A34}$$

In other words, the "attribute adjusted" number of visits to site i is $V_i/H(A_i)$. Now if the household selects the sites visited so as to minimise the cost of getting a given level of recreational services R then it will select the number of visits to each site so that the unit cost per visit of each site visited is equalised. This requires that,

$$p_i/H(A_i) = p_j/H(A_j) \tag{A35}$$

The terms on each side of (A35) are the price of a visit to a site adjusted for the attributes of that site. Since these are equalised across sites we can, by working with this attribute adjusted price, effectively look at one site at a time in examining the demand for visits. We can now write the minimum cost of obtaining a given level of recreational services R as C where:

$$C = C(p_i/H(A_i), R) \tag{A36}$$

Differentiating C with respect to p_i gives the demand function for V_i *given* R. R, however, can now be written as a function of the attribute adjusted prices and potential income Y. Substituting in for R in (A36) will give us an equation for V of the form:

$$V_i = V(p_i, H(A_i),Y) \tag{A37}$$

In estimating equation (A37) Y is usually replaced by household income. No data are available for the former and the error in using household income is not considered to be large. The specific form of the equation that is estimated is:

$$\log(V_i) = \alpha_0(A_i) + \alpha_1(A_i)p_i + \alpha_2(A_i)Y \tag{A38}$$

The α s are made functions of the site attributes A_i. (A38) is estimated in two stages. The first estimates the parameters α

for *each* i, so that the A_is are constant. The second stage estimates the parameters of the relationship between the α s and the elements of A.

$$\alpha_i = \beta_{i0} + \beta_{i1}a_{i1} + \beta_{i2}a_{i2} + ... \tag{A39}$$

The a_is are the elements of the vector A_i. The first stage has been estimated by least squares but this does not allow for the discreteness of the dependent variable or for truncation (see text for details). Maximum likelihood discrete estimation

methods are preferable. The second stage uses a generalised least squares estimator, which takes account of the relative precision of the estimates of the α s across sites.

The model we have outlined here has not looked at the choice of time spent on site explicitly. If this is included in p_i then we should simultaneously estimate an equation for the length of time spent at site i. In principle this can be done, but it does require data on onsite time and it involves the use of simultaneous equation methods.

VALUING HEALTH IN THE CONTEXT OF THE THEORY OF CONSUMER CHOICE

Section 5.2(iv) indicated that dose-response relationships tend to neglect the theory of consumer choice. Cropper (1981) and Gerking and Stanley (1986) have produced models in which individuals are regarded as producing health "capital", some of which offsets the effects of pollution.
The individual's utility function is:

$$U = U(X,H) \qquad (A40)$$

where X is goods and H is the stock of health capital. In turn, H is determined by a production function:

$$H = H(M,E,V) \qquad (A41)$$

where M is (non utility generating) medical care, E is environmental quality, and V is other variables affecting H. The budget constraint allows for both prices and time spent:

$$q_i = p_i + W.T_i \qquad (A42)$$

where q_i is the "full price" of the ith good, P_i is the market price, W is the wage rate and T_i is the time spent consuming one unit of the ith good.

The budget constraint is then written:

$$W.T + Y = X._{qX} + M._{qM} + W.T_{0L} \qquad (A43)$$

W.T + Y is "full income" and T_L is time lost due to illness. Equation (A40) is then maximised subject to (A41) to (A43). A measure of the compensating variation (the marginal willingness to pay for environmental quality) is then:

$$\delta Y/\delta E = [-\delta H/\delta E.\delta q/\delta E]/[\delta H/\delta M] \qquad (A44)$$

or

$$Y_E = [-H_E.q_M]/[H_M] \qquad (A45)$$

Observe that:

i) Y_E, the individual's willingness to pay for better environmental quality, increases as the improvement in health associated with that quality increases (H_E),

ii) Y_E is related to the health production function (via H_E and H_M) and not to any dose-response function,

iii) M is chosen by the consumer, whereas in the dose-response relationship, M is exogenous.

A SIMPLIFIED MODEL OF THE KRUTILLA-FISHER APPROACH
TO IRREVERSIBILITY

This outline of the Krutilla-Fisher approach follows that given by Porter (1982). It uses perpetuities rather than finite periods. Consider a development project costing $1. Let the net benefits of the development be $D per annum. Then the present value of the development is PV(D) where:

$$PV(D) = -1 + \int_0^\infty D\, e^{-rt}\, dt. \qquad (A46)$$

r is the discount rate and the integration is over an infinite interval. Next we assume that the development benefits are subject to a rate of "technological decay", k, (see the text), so that:

$$D_t = D_0\, e^{-kt} \qquad (A47)$$

where D_0 is the development benefit in year 0. Now turning to the preservation benefits, we will have:

$$PV(P) = \int_0^\infty P e^{-rt}\, dt. \qquad (A48)$$

and

$$P_t = P_0\, e^{gt} \qquad (A49)$$

where g is the rate of growth of preservation benefits. Bringing equations (A46) to (A49) together and solving the integrals gives:

$$NPV(D) = -1 + D/(r+k) - P/(r-g) \qquad (A50)$$

Equation (A50) implies that the net present value of development benefits will be positive if and only if the discount rate lies in a particular range. At low rates, g tends to push the preservation benefits up high so that the development project is not worthwhile. High rates tend to discriminate in the usual way, by reducing the development benefits. Porter shows that comparatively low values of g and k have the effect of pushing the development project into the region of being unacceptable.

BIBLIOGRAPHY

Abelson P.W. and Markandya A. (1985), "The Interpretation of Capitalized Hedonic Prices in a Dynamic Environment", *Journal of Environmental Economics and Management*, Vol. 12, pp. 195-206.

Adams R.M., Callaway J.M. and McCarl B.A. (1986), "Pollution, Agriculture and Social Welfare: The Case of Acid Deposition", *Canadian Journal of Agricultural Economics*, Vol. 34, (March), pp. 1-19.

Adams R.M., Crocker T.D. and Katz R.W. (1984), "The Adequacy of Natural Science Information in Economic Assessments of Pollution Control: A Bayesian Methodology", *Review of Economics and Statistics*, Vol. 66, pp. 568-575.

Adams R.M., Crocker T.D. and Thanavibulchai N. (1982), "An Economic Assessment of Air Pollution Damages to Selected Annual Crops in Southern California", *Journal of Environmental Economics and Management*, Vol. 9, pp. 42-58.

Adams R.M. and McCarl B.A. (1985), "Assessing the Benefits of Alternative Ozone Standards on Agriculture: The Role of Response Information", *Journal of Environmental Economics and Management*, Vol. 12, pp. 264-276.

Andrews R.N. (1984), "Economics and Environmental Decision Making: Past and Present", in V. Kerry Smith (ed.), *Environmental Policy under Reagan's Executive Order: The Role of Benefit-Cost Analysis*, University of North Carolina Press, Chapel Hill.

Arnould R. and Nichols L. (1983), "Wage Risk Premiums and Workers' Compensation: A Refinement of Estimates of Compensating Wage Differential", *Journal of Political Economy*, Vol. 91, pp.332-340.

Banford N., Knetch J. and Mauser G. (1977), "Compensating and Equivalent Measures of Consumer's Surplus: Further Survey Results", Department of Economics, Simon Fraser University, Vancouver.

Bentkover J.D., Covello V.T. and Munpower J. (1986). *Benefit Assessment: The State of the Art*, D. Reidel, Dordrecht.

Bidwell R. (1986), "Benefits Assessment in the Context of Environmental Decision-Making", Paper presented to the OECD-CEE Workshop on the Benefits of Environmental Policy and Decision-Making, Avignon, October.

Binkley C.S. and Hanemann W.M. (1978), "The Recreation Benefits of Water Quality Improvement: Analysis of Day Trips in an Urban Setting", US Environmental Protection Agency, Washington, D.C.

Bishop R.C. (1982), "Option Value: An Exposition and Extension", *Land Economics*, Vol. 58, No. 1, pp. l-l5.

Bishop R.C. and Heberlein T.A. (1979), "Measuring Values of Extra-Market Goods: Are Indirect Measures Biased?",

American Journal of Agricultural Economics, Vol. 6, December, pp. 926-930.

Bishop R., Heberlein T., and Kealey M.J. (1983), "Contingent Valuation of Environmental Assets: Comparisons with a Simulated Market", *Natural Resources Journal*, Vol. 23, July, pp. 6l9-633.

Bishop R., Heberlein T., Welsh M. and Baumgartner R. (1984), "Does Contingent Valuation Work? Results of the Sandhill Experiment", Department of Economics, University of Wisconsin, -mimeo-.

Boyle K., Bishop R. and Walsh M. (1985), "Starting Point Bias in Contingent Valuation Bidding Games", *Land Economics*, Vol. 61, pp. 188-194.

Brookshire D., Randall A. and Stoll R. (1980), "Valuing Increments in and Decrements in Natural Resource Service Flows", *American Journal of Agricultural Economics*, Vol. 62, 3, pp. 478-488.

Brookshire D., Thayer M., Tischirhart J., and Schulze W.D. (1985), "A Test of the Expected Utility Model: Evidence from Earthquake Risks", *Journal of Political Economy*, Vol. 93, pp. 369-389.

Brookshire D., Schulze W.D. and Thayer M. (1985), "Some Unusual Aspects of Valuing a Unique Natural Resource", University of Wyoming, -mimeo-.

Brookshire D., Thayer M., Schulze W. and D'Arge R. (1982), "Valuing Public Goods: a Comparison of Survey and Hedonic Approaches", *American Economic Review*, Vol. 72, No. l, pp. 165-171.

Broome J. (1979), "Trying to Value a Life", *Journal of Public Economics*, Vol. 9, pp. 91-100.

Brown J. and Rosen M. (1982), "On the Estimation of Structural Hedonic Price Models", *Econometrica*, Vol. 50, pp. 765-768.

Buchanan J.M. and Faith R.L. (1979), "Trying Again to Value a Life", *Journal of Public Economics*, Vol. l0, pp. 245-248.

Cesario F.J. (1976), "Value of Time in Recreation Benefit Studies", *Land Economics*, Vol. 52, pp. 32-41.

Chappie M. and Lave L. (1983), "The Health Effects of Air Pollution; a Reanalysis", *Journal of Urban Economics*, Vol. 12, pp. 346-376.

Chinn, S., du V. Florey, C., Baldwin, I. and Gorgol, M. (1981), "The Relation of Mortality in England and Wales 1969-1973 to Measurements of Air Pollution", *Journal of Epidemiology and Community Health*, Vol. 35, pp. 174-179.

Ciccheti C.J., Fisher A.C. and Kerry Smith V. (1976), "An Economic Evaluation of a Generalized Consumer Surplus

Measure: The Mineral King Controversy", *Econometrica*, Vol. 44, pp. 1259-1276.

Clawson M. (1959), *Methods of Measuring the Demand for and Value of Outdoor Recreation*, Reprint No. 10, Resources for the Future Inc., Washington, D.C.

Clawson M. and Knetch J.L. (1966), *Economics of Outdoor Recreation*, Resources for the Future Inc., Washington, D.C.

Cohon (1978), *Multi-objective Programming and Planning*, Academic Press, New York.

Cooper B.S. and Rice D.P. (1976), "The Economic Costs of Illness Revisited", *Social Security Bulletin*, Vol. 39, pp. 21-36.

Coursey D.L., Schulze W.D. and Hovis J. (1983), *A comparison of Alternative Valuation Mechanisms for Non Market Commodities*, Unpublished Manuscript, University of Wyoming.

Coursey D.L., Brookshire D., Gerking S., Anderson D., Schulze W. and Fisher A. (1985), *Laboratory Experimental Economics as a Tool for Measuring Public Policy Values*: Volume 1 of *Experimental Methods for Assessing Environmental Benefits*, US Environmental Protection Agency, Contract ≠CR-81107-01-0, Washington, D.C.

Crocker T.D. (1985), "Economic Impact of Acid Rain", Statement Before Select Committee on Environment and Public Works, US Senate.

Crocker T.D., Cummings R. and Forster B. (1985), *An Updating of Earlier Efforts to Estimate the National Benefits of Controlling Acid Precipitation*: Volume III of *Methods Development in Measuring Benefits of Environmental Improvements*, US Environmental Protection Agency, Washington, D.C.

Crocker T.D. and Forster B.A. (1985), "Some Economic Implications of Alternative Biological and Chemical Explanations of the Impacts of Acid Deposition on Forest Ecosystems", Paper presented at International Symposium on Acidic Precipitation, Muskoka, Canada.

Crocker T.D., Schulze W., Ben-David S. and Kneese A. (1979), *Methods Development for Assessing Air Pollution Control Benefits* Vol. 1: *Experiments in the Economics of Air Pollution Epidemiology*, US Environmental Protection Agency, Report EPA-600/5-79-001A, Washington, D.C.

Cropper M.L. (1981), "Measuring the Benefits from Reduced Morbidity", *American Economic Review Papers and Proceedings*, Vol. 71, No. 2, pp. 235-340.

Cummings R., Brookshire D. and Schulze W. (1984), *Valuing Environmental Goods: A State of the Arts Assessment of the Contingent Valuation Method*, Vols. 1A and 1B, Report to the Office of Policy Analysis, US Environmental Protection Agency, Washington, D.C.

Desvousges W.H., Smith V.K., and McGivney M.P. (1983), "A Comparison of Alternative Approaches for Estimating Recreation and Related Benefits of Water Quality Improvements", US Environmental Protection Agency, Washington, D.C.

Dickens W.T. (1984), "Differences Between Risk Premiums in Union and Non-Union Wages and the Case for Occupational Safety Regulation", *American Economic Review*, Vol. 74, No. 2, pp. 320-323.

Dillingham A. (1979), *The Injury Risk Structure of Occupations and Wages*, Ph.D. dissertation, Cornell University.

Economic Commission for Europe (1982), Effects of Sulphur Compounds on Materials, Including Historic and Cultural Monuments, Draft Report, ENV/IEB/WG1. UN ECE, Geneva.

Ewers H.-J. (1986), "Die Kosten der Umweltverschmutzung – Probleme ihrer Erfassung, Quantifizierung und Bewertung". In: *Kosten der Umweltverschmutzung*, Berichte 7/86 des Umweltbundesamtes, Berlin, S. 9ff.

Fischoff B., Lichtenstein S., Slovic P., Derby S. and Keeney R., (1981), *Acceptable Risk*, Cambridge University Press, Cambridge.

Freeman A.M. (1974), "On Estimating Air Pollution Control Benefits from Land Value Studies", *Journal of Environmental Economics and Management*, Vol. 1, No. 1, pp. 74-83.

Freeman A.M. (1979a), "Hedonic Prices, Property Values and Measuring Environmental Benefits", *Scandinavian Journal of Economics*, Vol. 81, pp. 154-173.

Freeman A.M. (1979b), The *Benefits of Environmental Improvement, Theory and Practice*, Johns Hopkins University Press, Baltimore.

Freeman A.M. (1982), *Air and Water Pollution Control: A Benefit-Cost Assessment*, Wiley, New York, 1982.

Garcia P., Dixon B.L. and Mjelde J.W. (1986), "Measuring the Benefits of Environmental Change Using a Duality Approach: The Case of Ozone and Illinois Cash Grain Farms", *Journal of Environmental Economics and Management*, Vol. 13, pp. 69-80.

Gerkin S. and Schulze W. (1981), 'What Do We Know About Benefits of Reduced Mortality from Air Pollution Control?', *American Economic Review*, Vol. 71, No. 2, May.

Gerking S. and Stanley L. (1986), "An Economic Analysis of Air Pollution and Health: The Case of St. Louis", *Review of Economics and Statistics*, Vol. LXVIII, No. 1, pp. 115-121.

Graves R. and Krumm R. (1981), *Health and Air Quality*, American Enterprise Institute for Public Policy Research, Washington, DC.

Gregory R. (1986), "Interpreting Measures of Economic Loss: Evidence from Contingent Valuation and Experimental Studies", *Journal of Environmental Economics and Management*, Vol. 13, pp. 325-337.

Haigh J., Harrison D. and Nichols A. (1984), "Benefit-Cost Analysis of Environmental Regulation Case Sudies of Hazardous Air Pollutants", *The Harvard Environmental Law Review*, Vol. 8, No. 2, pp. 395-434.

Halvorsen R. and Pollakowski H. (1981), "Choice of Functional Forms for Hedonic Price Equations", *Journal of Urban Economics*, Vol. 10, pp. 37-49.

Halvorsen R. and Ruby M. (1981), *Benefit-Cost Analysis of Air Pollution Control*, D.C. Health and Co., Lexington, Massachussetts.

Hammack J. and Brown G. (1974), *Waterfowl and Wetlands: Toward Bioeconomic Analysis*, Johns Hopkins University Press, Baltimore.

Heinz I. (1986), "Zur ökonomischen Bewertung von Materialschäden durch Luftverschmutzung". In: *Kosten der Umweltverschmutzung*, Berichte 7/86 des Umweltbundesamts, Berlin, S. 83ff.

Horowitz J.L. (1985), *Inferring Willingness to Pay for Housing Amenities from Residential Property Values*. Report EPA 600/7-85-034.

Horst R.L., Manuel E.H., Black R.M., Tapiero J.K., Brennan K.M. and Duff M.C. (1986), "A Damage Function Assessment of Building Materials: The Impact of Acid Deposition", Mathtech Inc., Princeton, New Jersey, Report prepared for the EPA, Washington, D.C.

Hotelling H. (1949), "The Economics of Public Recreation – An Economic Survey of the Monetary Evaluation of Recreation in the National Parks", A Report by R.A. Prewitt, National Parks Service, Washington, D.C.

Jones-Lee M. (1979), "Trying to Value a Life – Why Broome Does not Sweep Clean", *Journal of Public Economics*, Vol. 10, pp. 249-256.

Jones-Lee M.W., Hammerton M., and Philips P.R. (1985), "The Value of Safety: Results of a National Sample Survey", *Economic Journal*, Vol. 95, pp. 49-72.

Kahnemann D. and Tversky A. (1979), "Prospect Theory: An Analysis of Decision Making Under Risk", *Econometrica*. Vol. 47, pp. 263-291.

Klepper S. and Leamer E.E. (1984), "Consistent Sets of Estimates for Regressions with Errors in All Variables", *Econometrica*, Vol. 51, pp. 163-183.

Kneese A.V. (1984), *Measuring the Benefits of Clean Air and Water*, Resources for the Future Inc., Washington, D.C.

Knetsch J. and Davis R.K. (1966), "Comparisons of Methods for Recreation Evaluation" in A. Kneese and S. Smith (eds), *Water Research*, Johns Hopkins University Press, Baltimore.

Knetsch J. and Sinden J. (1984), "Willingness to Pay and Compensation Demanded: Experimental Evidence of an Unexpected Disparity in Measures of Value", *Quarterly Journal of Economics*, Vol. 99, pp. 507-521.

Kopp R.J., Vaughan N.J. and Hazilla M. (1984), "Agricultural Sector Benefits Analysis for Ozone: Methods Evaluation and Demonstration", Office of Air Quality Planning and Standards, Raleigh, N.C.

Krutilla J. and Fisher A. (1975), *The Economics of Natural Environments: Studies in the Valuation of Commodity and Amenity Resources*, Johns Hopkins University Press, Baltimore.

Lave L. and Seskin E. (1973), "An Analysis of the Association between US Mortality and Air Pollution", *Journal of the American Statistical Association*, Vol. 68, No. 342, pp. 284-290.

Lave L. and Seskin E. (1977), *Air Pollution and Human Health*, Johns Hopkins University Press, Baltimore.

Lipfert F.W. (1979), 'On the Evaluation of Air Pollution Control Benefits', The Benefits Estimation Panel, (US) National Commission on Air Quality, Washington, D.C.

Lipfert F.W. (1984), "Air Pollution and Mortality: Specification Searches Using SMSA-Based Data", *Journal of Environmental Economics and Management*, Vol. 11, pp. 371-382.

Litai D. (1980), *A risk Comparison Methodology for the Assessment of Acceptable Risk*, Ph.D. Thesis, Massachusetts Institute of Technology.

MacLennan D. (1977), "Some Thoughts on the Nature and Purpose of House Price Studies", *Urban Studies*, Vol. 14, pp. 59-71.

Marin A. and Psacharopoulos G. (1982), "The Reward for Risk in the Labor Market: Evidence from the United Kingdom and a Reconciliation with Other Studies", *Journal of Political Economy*, Vol. 90, No. 4, pp. 827-853.

Ministry of Housing and Environment, Netherlands (1986), "The Benefits of Environmental Policy in the Netherlands", Excerpts from Recent Dutch Studies, July 1986.

Mishan E. (1981), "The Value of Trying to Value a Life", *Journal of Public Economics*, Vol. 15, pp. 133-137.

Mitchell R.C. and Carson R.T. (1981), *An Experiment in Determining Willingness to Pay for National Water Quality Improvement*, Draft Report to US Environmental Protection Agency, Washington, D.C.

Needleman L. (1979), "The Valuation of Changes in the Risk of Death by Those at Risk", University of Waterloo, Working Paper 103.

Nelson J.P. (1978a), *Economic Analysis of Transportation Noise Abatement*, Ballinger, Cambridge, Mass.

Nelson J.P. (1978b), "Residential Choice, Hedonic Prices and the Demand for Urban Air Quality", *Journal of Urban Economics*, Vol. 5, July, pp. 357-369.

Nelson J.P. (1980), "Airports and Property Values: A Survey of Recent Evidence", *Journal of Transport Economics and Policy*, XIV, pp. 37-52.

Nelson J.P. (1982), "Highway Noise and Property Values: A Survey of Recent Evidence", *Journal of Transport Economics and Policy*, XVI, pp. 117-130.

Norton G. (1984), *Resource Economics*, Arnold, London.

OECD (1982), *Benefits of Environmental Policies as Avoided Damage*, Draft Document prepared for the Environment Committee Group of Economic Experts, unrevised.

OECD (1985), "Environmental Policies: a Source of Jobs?", in *Environment and Economics*, OECD, Paris.

OECD (1985), *The Macroeconomic Impact of Environmental Expenditure*.

Olson C. (1981), "An Analysis of Wage Differentials Received by Workers on Dangerous Jobs", *Journal of Human Resources*, Vol. 16, pp. 167-185.

Opschoor J.B. (1986), "A Review of Monetary Estimates of Benefits of Environmental Improvements in the Netherlands", for OECD-CEE Workshop on Benefits of Environmental Policy and Decision-Making, Avignon, October.

Ostro B. (1983), "The Effects of Air Pollution on Work Loss and Morbidity", *Journal of Environmental Economics and Management*, Vol. 10, pp. 371-382.

Ostro, B. (1987), "Air Pollution and Morbidity Revisited: a Specification Test", *Journal of Environmental Economics and Management*, Vol. 14, No. 1, pp. 87-98.

Page T. (1977), *Conservation and Economic Efficiency*, Johns Hopkins University Press for Resources for the Future, Baltimore and London.

Page T. (1986), "The Discount Rate and Intergenerational Equity", Caltech, -mimeo-.

Pearce D.W. (1976), "The Limits of Cost-Benefit Analysis as a Guide to Environmental Policy", *Kyklos*, Vol. 29, pp. 97-112.

Pearce D.W. (1980), "The Social Incidence of Environmental Costs and Benefits", in T.K. O'Riordan and R.K. Turner (eds), *Progress in Resource Management and Environmental Planning*, Vol. 2, John Wiley, Chichester.

Pearce D.W. and Nash C.A. (1981), *The Social Appraisal of Projects*, Macmillan, London.

Pickles, J.H. (1986), "Health Risks and Air Pollution – Error Analysis for a Cross-Sectional Mortality Study", *Risk Analysis*, Vol. 6, No. 2, pp. 203-212.

Pommerehne W. (1986) in *Offre et Financement des Services Publics Locaux*, Gurgat P. et Jeanrenauds, C. (eds), Economica, Paris.

Porter P. (1982), "The New Approach to Wilderness Preservation through Benefit-Cost Analysis", *Journal of Environmental Economics and Management*, Vol. 9, pp. 59-80.

Portney P. and Mullahy J. (1983), *Ambient Ozone and Human Health: An Epidemiological Analysis*, 2 Volumes, US Environmental Protection Agency, Office of Air Quality Planning and Standards.

Rosen S. (1979), "Wage-based Indexes of Urban Quality of Life", in *Current Issues in Urban Economics*, P. Mieszkowski and M. Strazheim, Eds., Johns Hopkins University Press, Baltimore and London.

Rosen S. (1981), "Valuing Health Risk", *American Economic Review: Papers and Proceedings*, Vol. 71, No. 2, pp. 241-245.

Rowe R.D., d'Arge R. and Brookshire D. (1980), "An Experiment on the Economic Value of Visibility", *Journal of Environmental Economics and Management*, Vol. 7, pp. 1-17.

Saddler H., Bennett J., Reynolds I. and Smith B. (1980), *Public Choice in Tasmania: Aspects of the Lower Gordon River Hydro-Electric Development Proposal*, Centre for Resource and Environmental Studies, Australian National University, Canberra.

Samuelson P.A. (1954), "Pure Theory of Public Expenditure", *Review of Economics and Statistics*, Vol. 36, pp. 387-389.

Schmalensee R. (1972), "Option Demand and Consumer's Surplus: Valuing Price Changes under Uncertainty", *American Economic Review*, Vol. 262, pp. 813-824.

Schmalensee R. (1975), "Option Demand and Consumer's Surplus: Reply", *American Economic Review*, Vol. 65, pp. 737-9.

Schulz W. (1985a), *Bessere Luft, Was ist sie uns wert? Eine Gesellschaftliche Bedarfs-Analyse auf der Basis Individueller Zahlungs-Bereitschaft*, Technical University of Berlin, Germany, July.

Schulz W. (1985b), *Der Monetäre Wert Besserer Luft*, Frankfurt, Bern and New York.

Schulz W. (1986), "A Survey on the Status of Research Concerning the Evaluation of Benefits of Environmental Policy in the Federal Republic of Germany", OECD-CEE Workshop on the Benefits of Environmental Policy and Decision-Making, Avignon, october.

Schulze W.D., d'Arge R.C. and Brookshire D.S. (1981), "Valuing Environmental Commodities: Some Recent Experiments", *Land Economics*, Vol. 57, pp. 151-172.

Schulze W., Brookshire D., Walther E., MacFarland K., Thayer M., Whitworth R., Ben-David S., Malm W. and Molenar J. (1983), "The Economic Benefits of Preserving Visibility in the National Parklands of the Southwest", *Natural Resources Journal*, Vol. 23, January, pp. 149-173.

Seller C., Stoll J. and Chavas J-P. (1985), "Validation of Empirical Measures of Welfare Change: A Comparison of Non-Market Techniques", *Land Economics*, Vol. 61, pp. 156-175.

Seskin E. (1979), "An Analysis of Some Short-Term Health Effects of Air Pollution in the Washington, D.C. Metropolitan Areas", *Journal of Urban Economics*, Vol. 6, pp. 275-291.

Sinclair W.S. (1976), "The Economic-Social Impact of the Kemano II Hydroelectric Project on British Columbia's Fisheries Resources", Department of the Environment, Fisheries and Marine Service, Vancouver.

Smith R. (1974), "The Feasibility of an Injury Tax Approach to Occupational Safety", *Law and Contemporary Problems*, Vol. 38, pp. 730-44.

Smith V.K. (1983), "The Role of Site and Job Characteristics in Hedonic Wage Models", *Journal of Urban Economics*, Vol. 13, pp. 296-321.

Smith V.K. (1986), "A Conceptual Overview of the Foundations of Benefit-Cost Analysis", in Bentkover *et al.*, *Benefit Assessment: The State of the Art*, D. Reidel, Dordrecht.

Smith V.K. and Gilbert C.S. (1984), "The Implicit Valuation of Risks to Life: A Comparative Analysis", *Economic Letters*, Vol. 16, pp. 393-399.

Smith V.K. and Desvousges W.H. (1985), "The Generalised Travel Cost Model and Water Quality Benefits: A Reconsideration", *Southern Economic Journal*, Vol. 52, pp. 371-382.

Strand J. (1981), "Valuation of Fresh Water Fish as a Public Good in Norway", Institute of Economics, University of Oslo, Oslo, -mimeo-.

Thaler R. (1980), "Toward a Positive Theory of Consumer Choice", *Journal of Economic Behaviour and Organisation*, Vol. 1, pp. 39-60.

Thaler R. and Rosen S. (1976), "The Value of Saving a Life: Evidence from the Labor Market", in N. Terleckyz (ed.), *Household Production and Consumption*, Columbia University Press, New York.

Thayer M. (1981), "Contingent Valuation Techniques for Assessing Environmental Impacts: Further Evidence", *Journal of Environmental Economics and Management*, Vol. 8, pp. 27-44.

Thibodeau L.A., *et al.* (1980), 'Air Pollution and Human Health: a Review and Reanalysis', *Environmental Health Perspectives*, 34, February.

Ulph A. (1982), 'The Role of Ex Ante and Ex Post Decisions in the Value of Life', *Journal of Public Economics*, Vol. 18, pp. 265-276.

Umweltbundesamt (1986), *Kosten der Umweltverschmutzung*. Procedings of a Symposium held in Bonn, 1985, Erich Schmidt Verlag, Umweltbundesamt Berichte, Berlin.

Veljanovski C. (1980), "The Economic Approach to Law: A Critical Introduction", *British Journal of Law and Society*, Vol. 7, No. 2, pp. 158-193.

Veljanovski C. (1981), *Regulating Industrial Accidents: An Economic Analysis of Market and Legal Responses*, Ph.D. thesis, University of York.

Violette D. and Chestnut L. (1983), *Valuing Reductions in Risks: A Review of The Empirical Estimates*, United States

Environmental Protection Agency, Washington, D.C., Report EPA-230-05-83-002.

Viscusi W.K. (1978a), "Health Effects and Earnings Premiums for Job Hazards", *Review of Economics and Statistics*, Vol. 60, pp. 408-416.

Viscusi W.K. (1978b), "Labour Market Valuations of Life and Limb: Empirical Evidence and Policy Implications", *Public Policy*, Vol. 26, pp. 359-386.

Viscusi W.K. (1986), "The Valuation of Risks to Life and Health: Guidelines for Policy Analysis", in Bentkover *et al.*

(eds.), *Benefit Assessment: The State of the Art*, D. Reidel, Dordrecht.

Watson W. and Jaksch J. (1982), "Air Pollution: Household Soiling and Consumer Welfare Losses", *Journal of Environmental Economics and Management*, Vol. 9, pp. 248-262.

Wicke L. (1986), *Die Öklogischen Milliarden. Das kostet die Zerstörte Umwelt – So Können Wir Sie Retten.* Kösel-Munich.

Zeleny M. (1982), *Multiple Criteria Decision making*, Wiley, New York.

WHERE TO OBTAIN OECD PUBLICATIONS
OÙ OBTENIR LES PUBLICATIONS DE L'OCDE

ARGENTINA - ARGENTINE
Carlos Hirsch S.R.L.,
Florida 165, 4º Piso,
(Galeria Guemes) 1333 Buenos Aires
Tel. 33.1787.2391 y 30.7122

AUSTRALIA - AUSTRALIE
D.A. Book (Aust.) Pty. Ltd.
11-13 Station Street (P.O. Box 163)
Mitcham, Vic. 3132   Tel. (03) 873 4411

AUSTRIA - AUTRICHE
OECD Publications and Information Centre,
4 Simrockstrasse,
5300 Bonn (Germany)   Tel. (0228) 21.60.45
Gerold & Co., Graben 31, Wien 1 Tel. 52.22.35

BELGIUM - BELGIQUE
Jean de Lannoy,
Avenue du Roi 202
B-1060 Bruxelles   Tel. (02) 538.51.69

CANADA
Renouf Publishing Company Ltd
1294 Algoma Road, Ottawa, Ont. K1B 3W8
Tel: (613) 741-4333
Stores:
61 rue Sparks St., Ottawa, Ont. K1P 5R1
Tel: (613) 238-8985
211 rue Yonge St., Toronto, Ont. M5B 1M4
Tel: (416) 363-3171
Federal Publications Inc.,
301-303 King St. W.,
Toronto, Ont. M5V 1J5   Tel. (416)581-1552
Les Éditions la Liberté inc.,
3020 Chemin Sainte-Foy,
Sainte-Foy, P.Q. GIX 3V6,   Tel. (418)658-3763

DENMARK - DANEMARK
Munksgaard Export and Subscription Service
35, Nørre Søgade, DK-1370 København K
Tel. +45.1.12.85.70

FINLAND - FINLANDE
Akateeminen Kirjakauppa,
Keskuskatu 1, 00100 Helsinki 10   Tel. 0.12141

FRANCE
OCDE/OECD
Mail Orders/Commandes par correspondance :
2, rue André-Pascal,
75775 Paris Cedex 16   Tel. (1) 45.24.82.00
Bookshop/Librairie : 33, rue Octave-Feuillet
75016 Paris
Tel. (1) 45.24.81.67 or/ou (1) 45.24.81.81
Librairie de l'Université,
12a, rue Nazareth,
13602 Aix-en-Provence   Tel. 42.26.18.08

GERMANY - ALLEMAGNE
OECD Publications and Information Centre,
4 Simrockstrasse,
5300 Bonn   Tel. (0228) 21.60.45

GREECE - GRÈCE
Librairie Kauffmann,
28, rue du Stade, 105 64 Athens   Tel. 322.21.60

HONG KONG
Government Information Services,
Publications (Sales) Office,
Information Services Department
No. 1, Battery Path, Central

ICELAND - ISLANDE
Snæbjörn Jónsson & Co., h.f.,
Hafnarstræti 4 & 9,
P.O.B. 1131 – Reykjavik
Tel. 13133/14281/11936

INDIA - INDE
Oxford Book and Stationery Co.,
Scindia House, New Delhi 110001
Tel. 331.5896/5308
17 Park St., Calcutta 700016   Tel. 240832

INDONESIA - INDONÉSIE
Pdii-Lipi, P.O. Box 3065/JKT.Jakarta
Tel. 583467

IRELAND - IRLANDE
TDC Publishers - Library Suppliers,
12 North Frederick Street, Dublin 1
Tel. 744835-749677

ITALY - ITALIE
Libreria Commissionaria Sansoni,
Via Benedetto Fortini 120/10,
Casella Post. 552
50125 Firenze   Tel. 055/645415
Via Bartolini 29, 20155 Milano   Tel. 365083
La diffusione delle pubblicazioni OCSE viene
assicurata dalle principali librerie ed anche da :
Editrice e Libreria Herder,
Piazza Montecitorio 120, 00186 Roma
Tel. 6794628
Libreria Hœpli,
Via Hœpli 5, 20121 Milano   Tel. 865446
Libreria Scientifica
Dott. Lucio de Biasio "Aeiou"
Via Meravigli 16, 20123 Milano   Tel. 807679

JAPAN - JAPON
OECD Publications and Information Centre,
Landic Akasaka Bldg., 2-3-4 Akasaka,
Minato-ku, Tokyo 107   Tel. 586.2016

KOREA - CORÉE
Kyobo Book Centre Co. Ltd.
P.O.Box: Kwang Hwa Moon 1658,
Seoul   Tel. (REP) 730.78.91

LEBANON - LIBAN
Documenta Scientifica/Redico,
Edison Building, Bliss St.,
P.O.B. 5641, Beirut   Tel. 354429-344425

**MALAYSIA/SINGAPORE -
MALAISIE/SINGAPOUR**
University of Malaya Co-operative Bookshop
Ltd.,
7 Lrg 51A/227A, Petaling Jaya
Malaysia   Tel. 7565000/7565425
Information Publications Pte Ltd
Pei-Fu Industrial Building,
24 New Industrial Road No. 02-06
Singapore 1953   Tel. 2831786, 2831798

NETHERLANDS - PAYS-BAS
SDU Uitgeverij
Christoffel Plantijnstraat 2
Postbus 20014
2500 EA's-Gravenhage   Tel. 070-789911
Voor bestellingen: Tel. 070-789880

NEW ZEALAND - NOUVELLE-ZÉLANDE
Government Printing Office Bookshops:
Auckland: Retail Bookshop, 25 Rutland Stseet,
Mail Orders, 85 Beach Road
Private Bag C.P.O.
Hamilton: Retail: Ward Street,
Mail Orders, P.O. Box 857
Wellington: Retail, Mulgrave Street, (Head
Office)
Cubacade World Trade Centre,
Mail Orders, Private Bag
Christchurch: Retail, 159 Hereford Street,
Mail Orders, Private Bag
Dunedin: Retail, Princes Street,
Mail Orders, P.O. Box 1104

NORWAY - NORVÈGE
Narvesen Info Center – NIC,
Bertrand Narvesens vei 2,
P.O.B. 6125 Etterstad, 0602 Oslo 6
Tel. (02) 67.83.10, (02) 68.40.20

PAKISTAN
Mirza Book Agency
65 Shahrah Quaid-E-Azam, Lahore 3 Tel. 66839

PHILIPPINES
I.J. Sagun Enterprises, Inc.
P.O. Box 4322 CPO Manila
Tel. 695-1946, 922-9495

PORTUGAL
Livraria Portugal, Rua do Carmo 70-74,
1117 Lisboa Codex   Tel. 360582/3

**SINGAPORE/MALAYSIA -
SINGAPOUR/MALAISIE**
See "Malaysia/Singapor". Voir
« Malaisie/Singapour »

SPAIN - ESPAGNE
Mundi-Prensa Libros, S.A.,
Castelló 37, Apartado 1223, Madrid-28001
Tel. 431.33.99
Libreria Bosch, Ronda Universidad 11,
Barcelona 7   Tel. 317.53.08/317.53.58

SWEDEN - SUÈDE
AB CE Fritzes Kungl. Hovbokhandel,
Box 16356, S 103 27 STH,
Regeringsgatan 12,
DS Stockholm   Tel. (08) 23.89.00
Subscription Agency/Abonnements:
Wennergren-Williams AB,
Box 30004, S104 25 Stockholm Tel. (08)54.12.00

SWITZERLAND - SUISSE
OECD Publications and Information Centre,
4 Simrockstrasse,
5300 Bonn (Germany)   Tel. (0228) 21.60.45
Librairie Payot,
6 rue Grenus, 1211 Genève 11
Tel. (022) 31.89.50
Maditec S.A.
Ch. des Palettes 4
1020 – Renens/Lausanne   Tel. (021) 635.08.65
United Nations Bookshop/Librairie des Nations-
Unies
Palais des Nations, 1211 – Geneva 10
Tel. 022-34-60-11 (ext. 48 72)

TAIWAN - FORMOSE
Good Faith Worldwide Int'l Co., Ltd.
9th floor, No. 118, Sec.2, Chung Hsiao E. Road
Taipei   Tel. 391.7396/391.7397

THAILAND - THAILANDE
Suksit Siam Co., Ltd., 1715 Rama IV Rd.,
Samyam Bangkok 5   Tel. 2511630
INDEX Book Promotion & Service Ltd.
59/6 Soi Lang Suan, Ploenchit Road
Patjumamwan, Bangkok 10500
Tel. 250-1919, 252-1066

TURKEY - TURQUIE
Kültur Yayinlari Is-Türk Ltd. Sti.
Atatürk Bulvari No: 191/Kat. 21
Kavaklidere/Ankara   Tel. 25.07.60
Dolmabahce Cad. No: 29
Besiktas/Istanbul   Tel. 160.71.88

UNITED KINGDOM - ROYAUME-UNI
H.M. Stationery Office,
Postal orders only: (01)873-8483
P.O.B. 276, London SW8 5DT
Telephone orders: (01) 873-9090, or
Personal callers:
49 High Holborn, London WC1V 6HB
Branches at: Belfast, Birmingham,
Bristol, Edinburgh, Manchester

UNITED STATES - ÉTATS-UNIS
OECD Publications and Information Centre,
2001 L Street, N.W., Suite 700,
Washington, D.C. 20036 - 4095
Tel. (202) 785.6323

VENEZUELA
Libreria del Este,
Avda F. Miranda 52, Aptdo. 60337,
Edificio Galipan, Caracas 106
Tel. 951.17.05/951.23.07/951.12.97

YUGOSLAVIA - YOUGOSLAVIE
Jugoslovenska Knjiga, Knez Mihajlova 2,
P.O.B. 36, Beograd   Tel. 621.992

Orders and inquiries from countries where
Distributors have not yet been appointed should be
sent to:
OECD, Publications Service, 2, rue André-Pascal,
75775 PARIS CEDEX 16.

Les commandes provenant de pays où l'OCDE n'a
pas encore désigné de distributeur doivent être
adressées à :
OCDE, Service des Publications. 2, rue André-
Pascal, 75775 PARIS CEDEX 16.

72380-1-1989

OECD PUBLICATIONS, 2, rue André-Pascal, 75775 PARIS CEDEX 16 - No. 44643 1988
PRINTED IN FRANCE
(97 88 07 1) ISBN 92-64-13182-5

DATE DUE

GAYLORD			PRINTED IN U.S.A.